BERKELEY'S
THREE DIALOGUES

Continuum *Reader's Guides*

Continuum's *Reader's Guides* are clear, concise and accessible introductions to classic works of philosophy. Each book explores the major themes, historical and philosophical context and key passages of a major philosophical text, guiding the reader toward a thorough understanding of often demanding material. Ideal for undergraduate students, the guides provide an essential resource for anyone who needs to get to grips with a philosophical text.

Aristotle's Nicomachean Ethics – Christopher Warne

Deleuze and Guattari's Capitalism and Schizophrenia – Ian Buchanan

Hegel's Philosophy of Right – David Rose

Heidegger's Being and Time – William Blattner

Hobbes's Leviathan – Laurie M. Johnson Bagby

Hume's Dialogues Concerning Natural Religion – Andrew Pyle

Hume's Enquiry Concerning Human Understanding – Alan Bailey and Dan O'Brien

Kant's Critique of Pure Reason – James Luchte

Kant's Groundwork for the Metaphysics of Morals – Paul Guyer

Locke's Essay Concerning Human Understanding – William Uzgalis

Locke's Second Treatise of Government – Paul Kelly

Mill's On Liberty – Geoffrey Scarre

Mill's Utilitarianism – Henry West

Nietzsche's On the Genealogy of Morals – Daniel Conway

Plato's Republic – Luke Purshouse

Spinoza's Ethics – Thomas J Cook

Wittgenstein's Philosophical Investigations – Eric James

Wittgenstein's Tractatus Logico Philosophicus – Roger M White

BERKELEY'S
THREE DIALOGUES

A Reader's Guide

AARON GARRETT

continuum

Continuum International Publishing Group
The Tower Building   80 Maiden Lane
11 York Road   Suite 704
London SE1 7NX   New York, NY 10038
www.continuumbooks.com

British Library Cataloguing-in-Publication Data
A catalogue record for this book is available from the British Library.

ISBN: 0 8264 9662 8/978 0 8264 9662 1 (hardback)
0 8264 9323 8/978 0 8264 9323 1 (paperback)

Typeset by Servis Filmsetting Ltd, Manchester
Printed and bound in Great Britain by
Cromwell Press Ltd, Trowbridge, Wiltshire

CONTENTS

LIST OF ABBREVIATIONS

WORKS BY BERKELEY

A – *Alciphron*
An – *Analyst*
D – *Three Dialogues between Hylas and Philonous*
DFM – *A Defence of Free–thinking in Mathematics*
L – *Letters*
M – *De Motu*
NTV – *Essay towards a New Theory of Vision*
NTVV – *New Theory of Vision Vindicated*
P – *A Treatise concerning the Principles of Human Knowledge: Part One*
PC – *Notebooks* (referred to by Luce as the 'Philosophical Commentaries')
PO – *Passive Obedience*
S – *Siris*

All quotations from Berkeley are taken from A.A. Luce and T.E. Jessop (eds), *The Works of George Berkeley Bishop of Cloyne* (nine volumes, London: Thomas Nelson & Sons, Ltd, 1948–57). When citing Berkeley I have cited the works by numbered paragraph when possible, which is in *Principles, Essay Towards a New Theory of Vision, Philosophical Commentaries, Passive Obedience, New Theory of Vision Vindicated*, the *Analyst, De Motu*, and *A Defence of Free–thinking in Mathematics*. When referring to the *Letters* I have given the number of the letter, the volume, and the page number. *Alciphron* is cited by dialogue and section. When there are no paragraph or section numbers (as with the *Dialogues*, and the editor's prefaces to the volumes, etc.), I have cited by volume and page (for example, II:135).

WORKS BY OTHERS

E – John Locke, *An Essay concerning Human Understanding*, ed. P. H. Nidditch (Oxford: Clarendon Press, 1975) (cited by book, chapter, and paragraph)

T – David Hume, *A Treatise of Human Nature*, ed David Fate Norton and Mary Norton (two volumes, Oxford: Oxford University Press, 2007) (cited by book, chapter, and paragraph)

PREFACE

First things first. It's pronounced 'Bar-klee'.

Instead of beginning by stating what the general purpose of this book is, I would like to say what it is not. It is not a novel reading of Berkeley, nor a strong interpretation that will solve outstanding problems in the secondary literature (although I will refer to relevant secondary literature throughout, and pronounce on it on the odd occasion). It is not a defence of Berkeley against his many opponents, although I hope it is a charitable reading. It is not an attempt to show that if we read Berkeley in just the right way many problems in contemporary philosophy can be dissolved. It is not written for professional philosophers or historians of philosophy.

It is an attempt to provide a general reader or an undergraduate student with the sort of information I would like to have had when first reading Berkeley's *Three Dialogues between Hylas and Philonous* [*Dialogues*]. The *Dialogues* speaks very well for itself: it is not turgid or difficult to read, but beautifully written and carefully crafted. This book provides context for understanding the *Dialogues*, by reference both to Berkeley's other works and to relevant historical and philosophical background. Because this is a book on a work by Berkeley and not a book on Berkeley's philosophy in general, the structure of this book mirrors and follows the structure of the *Dialogues*. I try in the notes to point readers to relevant literature and interesting debates and questions, but the main body of the text is quite straightforward. I summarize Berkeley's text a lot, but hopefully in a manner that is clarifying, edifying, and provides a guide for readers through twists and turns that seem to have little rationale.

The aspects of the book that are distinctive (if not novel) are a stress on the importance of morals and religion for Berkeley, and on the literary elements in the *Dialogues*. By 'morals' I do not mean a particular system of morals – although Berkeley had one – but rather very generally that that we should live a decent, believing life. That this was important for Berkeley and connected with his other philosophical goals is not controversial. That the *Dialogues* is a literary work is also indisputable. That the *Dialogues* are *better* understood by highlighting Berkeley's moral and religious interests and its literary turns is perhaps more controversial, but I hope not too much so.

I undertook to write the book because Berkeley was a philosopher I had never really warmed to, unlike Locke and Hume. I have since warmed to him vehemently, and the result has been great pleasure. Thanks to Robert Bristol, Walter Hopp, John McHugh, Elizabeth Robins and Ken Winkler.

CHAPTER ONE

CONTEXT

What is the relation between how the world appears to me and what the world *is* in and of itself? Is my experience of the world – as colourful, as sublime, as horrifying – reducible to natural laws and causes? Do my ideas represent things or states outside of me? How and what do my ideas represent? What is the relation between language, the mind and the world? And, not least of all, if a tree falls in a forest and no one hears it, does it make a sound? George Berkeley asked and tried to answer these and many other related questions in a number of works, including the work that this book will examine, *Three Dialogues between Hylas and Philonous* [*Dialogues*]. Berkeley's answers are philosophically exciting, rich, and often more provocative than the questions they respond to.

They are also connected to different questions, which today we don't usually think of as related to metaphysics, the theory of knowledge, and the philosophy of perception (the areas of philosophy which we primarily associate with Berkeley), but which were important for Berkeley and his contemporaries. Are there things that perhaps we shouldn't seek to know? Why? What is the connection between our theories about the physical constitution of the world and morals? And religion? And conduct? And the best sort of life? These questions are pressing for Berkeley in the *Dialogues* and in his other works, and in fact only by making sense of them can we fully understand how Berkeley viewed metaphysics, knowledge, and perception. This is the odd circumstance in which we find ourselves as historians of philosophy. We are interested in philosophers of the past because of the enduring questions they ask and the answers they give. But we can only really make sense of what they meant to say – as opposed to blindly projecting our present concerns onto the text – if we also know something about their context. This means considering explanations, interests, and justifications that are often quite remote from those which spur our initial inquiry.

We often also find that our initial interest in particular philosophers and in particular issues in philosophy has been guided by very recent history. Berkeley's theories of perception and ideas were a touchstone for a number of influential philosophers of the first half of the twentieth century. A.J. Ayer tried to rehabilitate Berkeley as a progenitor of the phenomenalist theory of perception by ridding him of God.[1] J.L. Austin and G.J. Warnock offered Berkeley as an example of the failure of a certain kind of phenomenalism and pushed us towards the analysis of ordinary language.[2] Without knowing it, and without even having read the authors involved, we glide along the tracks of a dominant interpretation (which doesn't mean that the interpretation is wrong).[3] This is a phenomenon that Berkeley understood very well. He thought that one of the main tasks of the philosopher was to challenge beliefs and intuitions which we take as obvious – for example, that we can see distance or that all of our senses have the same objects – but are in fact incoherent. In the *Dialogues* he set out to test many of the beliefs and intuitions of his fellow philosophers in a vigorous but civil discussion.

BIOGRAPHY

We owe the *Dialogues* to an extraordinary period of philosophical ferment, when the young Berkeley produced three masterpieces in brisk succession: the *Dialogues* was the last of the trio (1713), preceded by the *Essay towards a New Theory of Vision* (1709) [*New Theory of Vision*], and *A Treatise concerning the Principles of Human Knowledge: Part One* (1710) [*Principles*]. The first in the series of works, the *New Theory of Vision*, was modestly successful (although it would become more and more influential as the eighteenth century went on). All three works drew on ideas that Berkeley had written in two unpublished notebooks when he was 21 (1707). He had recently become a Fellow of Trinity College, had just been ordained a deacon of the Anglican church, and was very soon to be ordained a priest.[4] At just 24 years old, Berkeley was clearly a man on the rise, and the time seemed right for an audacious, even shocking, new book – the *Principles*. An entry in the *Notebooks* reads: 'I am young, I am an upstart, I am a pretender, I am vain, very well. I shall Endeavour patiently to bear up under the most lessening, villifying appelations the pride & rage of man can devise' (A §465).[5]

Berkeley published the *Principles* in 1710 and eagerly awaited reports from Sir John Percival, one of his closest friends and the dedicatee of the *New Theory of Vision*, as to how the book had been received. Percival responded:

> a physician of my acquaintance undertook to describe your person, and argued you must needs be mad, and that you ought to take remedies. A bishop pitied you that a desire and vanity of starting something new should put you on such an undertaking . . . Another told me an ingenious man ought not be discouraged from exercising his wit, and said Erasmus was not the worse thought for writing in praise of folly, but that you are not gone so far as a gentleman in town who asserts not only that there is no such thing as matter but that we have no being at all. My wife, who has all the good esteem and opinion of you that is possible from your just notions of marriage–happiness, desires to know if there be nothing but spirit and ideas, what you make of that part of the six days' creation which preceded man. (IX:10)

In a moving reply to his friend, Berkeley responded to the criticisms, admitting that he was 'not at all surprised to find that the name of my book should be entertained with ridicule and contempt by those who never examined what was in it, and want that common justice of trying before they condemn' (L 12, VIII:36). He was particularly disturbed that he had been taken not to believe what he wrote, as a wit; and that he might be thought to be a sceptic bent on denying not just matter but existence and God. He responded warmly to Lady Percival's query but was clearly stung by the rest, despite his promise to bear up patiently.

Worse, the *Principles* barely registered in the wider Republic of Letters (with a few notable exceptions).[6] There was little rage or vilification, despite the genius and audacity of the work. The reviews that did appear were negative, dismissive, and in some cases showed little evidence that the reviewers had done more than skim the book.

That the little response that was offered was negative, uncomprehending, and dismissive is not surprising, given that Berkeley argued for positions orthogonal to many commonly and deeply held beliefs. This may also explain why the book took a while to register: it was just a bit too far afield from the assumptions of his peers. Berkeley's bold arguments that matter does not exist are still best known today not from any direct acquaintance with the *Principles* and the *Dialogues,* but rather from Samuel Johnson's 'refutation' of his immaterialism more than 50 years after the works were published.[7] Even today, although the *Principles* and the *Dialogues* are considered philosophical masterpieces, Berkeley's arguments are generally viewed as questionable and sometimes ridiculous. Berkeley's central argument for idealism was considered to be the seedbed of the 'Worst Argument in the World' by David Stove, and he snidely referred to his reconstruction of Berkeley's argument as the 'Gem'.[8] Smug dismissal was even easier in the early eighteenth century when the young, relatively unknown Berkeley first presented his arguments.

Given his early success and promise, Berkeley must have been deflated by the failure of the *Principles.* Instead of publishing the promised second part,[9] he used his considerable literary skills to add many spoonfuls of sugar to the most important rejected medicine of the first part of the *Principles,* with hopes that his basic message could then be swallowed more easily.[10] One of Berkeley's major philosophical influences, the great French Cartesian Nicolas Malebranche, had written *Dialogues on Metaphysics* (1688), where he presented arguments and ideas from the earlier *Search after Truth* (1674–5) (with important additions and some changes) in dialogue form. Shaftesbury's *Characteristics* and Fontenelle's *Conversations on the Plurality Worlds* (1686) were extremely popular when Berkeley was writing, and both used dialogue. He had also become associated with the literary circles of Joseph Addison, Richard Steele, Jonathan Swift, and Alexander Pope – the great British writers who created the *Guardian*, the *Spectator*, the Scribeleran society and many other of the most influential writings and influential literary culture of the eighteenth century. In this company, Berkeley decided to try his hand at a more literary form.

Unfortunately, although the *Dialogues* is beautifully written, it proved little more popular than the *Principles,* and took 12 years to go to a second edition.[11] By contrast, his friend Addison's *Cato: A Tragedy* went through nine editions in the same year that Berkeley published the *Dialogues.* Berkeley only wrote brief works for nearly 20 years after the *Dialogues* appeared, although some of these were quite important (like the essay *De Motu* on motion, which addressed some undeveloped issues in his earlier works).[12]

Berkeley was extremely busy in the interim. He continued to travel extensively, studied, and jockeyed for the support of patrons and for good church posts. His financial fortunes changed when in 1723 he inherited a tidy sum of money from the estate of a friend and in 1734 he was given a good, lucrative post – the Dean of Derry. At around this time Berkeley undertook the extraordinary project of establishing a college in the New World: St. Paul's College in Bermuda. Newly married, he sailed to Rhode Island in 1729 in order to oversee the project. He settled in Middletown, preached in Newport, but never managed to get the college off the ground, returning to England in 1731. As a conservative Anglican minister he was initially sceptical of Rhode Island, a place noted for dissent, but gradually warmed to the inhabitants.[13] His farm was eventually given to Yale, and his library split between Harvard and Yale.

While in Rhode Island he appears to have worked on *Alciphron*, a dialogue on morals and religion against free thinkers or 'minute philosophers', which he published in 1732. Unlike the *Dialogues*, *Alciphron* (1732) was quite popular and went to a second edition in its first year of publication. It occasioned an amusing response from Bernard Mandeville[14] entitled *A Letter to Dion* (1732): Berkeley had savagely criticized Mandeville's *Fable of the Bees* in the *Alciphron,* and Mandeville responded by trying to demonstrate that Berkeley had not actually read the work in question. Two years later Berkeley was appointed Bishop of Cloyne in Ireland, providing the 'Bishop' in 'Bishop Berkeley'. The early 1730s was a bit of a renaissance for Berkeley and he produced a series of publications including the *Theory of Vision Vindicated and Explained* (1733), and the *Analyst* (1734) which attacked Newton's fluxion calculus.

Ten years later Berkeley published *Siris* (1744), a strange, metaphysical tract on the medical remedy tar-water, which he thought was a nearly universal cure. It was the most popular of his writings during his lifetime, went through at least six editions and numerous reprints in one year and was translated into French.[15] He published little of note between this and his death in 1753. His reputation had grown over the course of his life, and although few became convinced Berkeleyans, some of the most important philosophers of the mid and later eighteenth century were deeply influenced by Berkeley's *Principles*, the *Three Dialogues*, and *An Essay Towards a New Theory of Vision* – notably Hume and Thomas Reid. These three books, the latter two of which had been relatively ignored when published, have dominated discussions of Berkeley's philosophical work from the nineteenth century to the present day. The great critic Leslie Stephen wrote that Berkeley's *Dialogues* was 'the finest specimen in our language of the conduct of argument by dialogue'. Even if it is not the only candidate for 'finest specimen' – there's also Shaftesbury's 'The Moralists' and Hume's *Dialogues on Natural Religion* – it is one of the very best. The *Dialogues* is not *just* the *Principles* in dialogue form though. Lord Shaftesbury,[16] Berkeley's great British predecessor in writing philosophical dialogues, had stressed in his *Characteristics* that the way in which doctrines or concepts are presented is inseparable from their content. Although Berkeley pilloried Lord Shaftesbury in the dialogue *Alciphron* and elsewhere as an 'atheistical' man, the *Dialogues* married form and content in much the way that Shaftesbury had advocated.

Two distinct aspects of Berkeley's interconnection of form and meaning are evident from the outset of the *Dialogues*. The work begins with Philonous, Berkeley's stand–in, admiring the sights, smells, and sounds of a beautiful morning. We are invited as readers to remember similar sensuous experiences, pointing to the richness of the senses and the power of language, a theme of the *Dialogues*. Second, the dialogue form lets a reader engage in philosophy as an active participant: it allows for a different form of argumentation than a treatise. A skilfully written dialogue anticipates the objections that a reader will formulate and carefully counters them. Readers who further engage may formulate more serious criticisms, but if they are at all reasonable they will not just put the arguments aside on the basis of a quick and shallow objection. Given the dismissive reception of the *Principles*, the dialogue form seemed an appropriate way to present his philosophy. Berkeley probably hoped that by engaging with the *Three Dialogues* readers would come to see that their reasons for rejecting his doctrines were insufficient; that their common sense had been muddied by bad philosophy, scepticism and irreligion; and that the true common sense that Berkeley advocated is consistent with good philosophy and religion. Although few of Berkeley's readers come away as convinced Berkeleyans, many come away with a sense of the power and delight of clear, direct argument, and with a greater awareness of where some of the most important philosophical nerves are (and that they need pressing).

INFLUENCES

Berkeley was influenced by a number of his notable philosophical predecessors, in particular John Locke (1632–1704) and the great French synthesizer of Descartes and St. Augustine, Nicolas Malebranche (1638–1715).[17] Their influences on Berkeley took the form not of discipleship but of powerful, and normally respectful, critical engagement. The passage I quoted above about his expected villification for having published the *Principles* goes on thus: 'I do not pin my faith on the sleeve of any great man . . . I do not adhere to any opinion because it is an old one, a receiv'd one, a fashionable one, or one that I have spent much time in study and cultivation of.' A few sentences later, Berkeley further remarked: 'If in some things I differ from a Philosopher I profess to admire, 'tis for that very thing on account whereof I admire him, namely the love of truth' (PC § 467).

He was also influenced as a philosopher by writers who were not philosophers in the narrow sense. At the time he was writing and publishing the *Dialogues*, Berkeley socialized a great deal with Addison, Swift, Arbuthnot, Steele, Pope, and other popular writers and intellectuals. He thought particularly well of Addison's philosophical abilities – 'Mr Addison has the same talents in a high degree, and is likewise a great philosopher, having applied himself to speculative studies more than any of the wits that I know.' He was not alone in this admiration: Hume, and many other eighteenth-century philosophers, admired Addison greatly. Addison famously announced in *Spectator* 10 that 'It was said of Socrates, that he brought Philosophy down from Heaven, to inhabit among Men; and I shall be ambitious to have it said of me, that I have brought Philosophy out of Closets and Libraries, Schools and Colleges, to dwell in Clubs and Assemblies, at Tea-tables, and in Coffee-houses.'[18] At the same time, Addison criticized coffee-house philosophers for prattling on heretically while understanding (and meaning) little. Like Addison, Berkeley was critical of coffee-house philosophical culture,[19] and he also shared the goal of liberating philosophy from its many closets and returning it to ordinary, rational scrutiny and discussion.

Furthermore, there were other writers that Berkeley engaged with critically but who were less steady influences than opponents. Berkeley has a number of important affinities with Shaftesbury, who was a dominant influence on early eighteenth-century letters. For many intellectuals, Shaftesbury's embrace of Platonism and

Stoicism in a modern guise offered a playful, humanist, aestheticized, civically minded counterballast to Locke's austere empiricism. Like Shaftesbury, Berkeley recognized the importance of philosophical style, was drawn to holism, took a critical stance towards Locke on innatism, and had a strong attraction to Platonism. However, Berkeley was scandalized by what he took to be Shaftesbury's irreligious deism and criticized him for it in *Alciphron*.[20] Like almost all early modern philosophers, Berkeley was influenced by Hobbes and Descartes, although he normally rejected their doctrines when he engaged with them explicitly.[21] He took much more from Descartes than he admitted, but he was not an Irish Cartesian.

His relation to Newton was much more respectful. He criticized Newton's doctrines of absolute space and time, of motion, the calculus or doctrine of fluxions, and the Newton worship that led 'philomathematical infidels' to 'imitate the greatest man in his defects' (*DFM* 15). Although Berkeley admired Newton's genius and did not doubt that he was a deeply religious man, he thought that Newton used abstract forces like gravity in a way which tended to posit abstract metaphysical causes in the physical world. This then diminished the importance of God and spurred the deists and atheists.[22] Berkeley believed that Newton's great discoveries could be given a far better support than Newton himself had given.

Locke
The central influence, though, is Locke. *An Essay concerning Human Understanding* was considered a watershed for British and French philosophers of the eighteenth century, and Berkeley was no exception in his admiration for Locke. There are far more references to Locke in Berkeley's *Notebooks* than to any other thinker. But, true to his word, while being fully aware of the magnitude of his debt Berkeley did not pin his faith on Locke's sleeve. One of the later entries in his notebooks, which he intended for a preface, reads: 'I am no more to be reckon'd stronger than Locke than a pigmy should be reckon'd stronger than a Gyant because he could throw off the Molehill which lay upon him, & the Gyant could onely shake or shove the Mountain that oppresed him' (*PC* §678). The image is reminiscent of Newton's famous remark to Hooke that 'If I have seen further it is by standing on ye shoulders of giants', as well as of the bravado of the Lilliputians in *Gulliver's Travels* (published nearly 20 years later by Berkeley's friend Jonathan Swift). It also underscores

that Berkeley thought of himself as aiding Locke, and throwing off the mountain which oppressed him, even if his usual engagement with Locke was highly contentious. Berkeley was not the only British philosopher of the first quarter of the eighteenth century who had wished to rescue Locke from himself. Two of the most important British moral philosophers of the first half of the eighteenth century, Francis Hutcheson (1694–1746) and Joseph Butler (1692–1752), both saw themselves (albeit each quite differently) as extending Locke's theory of knowledge and mind in a way that refuted Locke's hedonistic theory of moral motivation. Berkeley was also concerned with the moral consequences of Locke's doctrines, and saw himself as rescuing Locke, the mostly careful philosopher of the understanding, from intermittent confusion and carelessness that opened his doctrines up to atheism, materialism and immoralism (despite Locke's theist intentions).

Berkeley took his methodological stance, his empiricism, and his basic concepts from Locke's *Essay Concerning Human Understanding*. In the opening chapters of the *Essay*, Locke argued against innate ideas, presenting an account of the understanding where all knowledge is either derived from the senses or from reflection on our minds. Plato, Augustine, Descartes, Henry More, and many of Locke's other predecessors had argued for innate ideas. Innate ideas were often a lynchpin in theories of knowledge that took mathematical knowledge as paradigmatic, going all the way back to Plato's demonstration in the *Meno* that if an uneducated slave-boy was capable of following a mathematical proof, this showed that mathematical knowledge must be innate. Locke's rejection of innate ideas was primarily methodological. By what standard could we possibly recognize that an idea is innate, i.e., what about the idea leads us to conclude it is innate? And, given that one can always provide an alternative empirical explanation of whatever it is about the idea that we take as a mark of its innateness, do we ever really need recourse to innateness as an explanation?

Once innate ideas had been dismissed, Locke spent much of the remainder of the *Essay* developing a doctrine of ideas and an account of how ideas result in understanding. As already mentioned, Locke famously argued for only two sources of ideas: experience and reflection. Berkeley was deeply influenced by Locke's methodological rigour, and by his attempts to set out precisely what understanding is of and what it is to understand. He made great use of Locke's strategy of limiting knowledge to sense experience and reflection on mental processes, and then, much like Locke, he used the limitation on knowledge acquisition to rule out competing explanations. But although Berkeley drew on the style of argument that Locke had used to rule out innate ideas, he still thought that Locke had erred by beginning the *Essay* with a critique of innate ideas. In opposing sense experience to innate ideas Locke set up an opposition between 'knowledge from inside the mind', and 'knowledge of the world outside the mind', which took resemblances between ideas and an external world that they represent as the anchor for more complex knowledge. This was further interconnected with the distinction between simple and complex ideas, where simple ideas represented simple qualities that were then compounded into complex ideas. In his notebooks Berkeley remarks that Locke should have begun instead by considering the topics of Book III of the *Essay*: language, essence, and substance (*PC* 717). I will return to this passage in the section on abstract ideas, because I think it is important for understanding where Berkeley thought Locke had erred. It shows as well that Berkeley's concern with language was also deeply Lockean – in particular, it is related to Locke's idea (which spurred him into writing the *Essay*) that the reform of language was a necessary condition for proper philosophy.

Given the importance of Locke for Berkeley, I will discuss Locke's ideas again and again. For now, let's consider a few examples of how Berkeley developed from this critical engagement with Locke. At the beginning of 'Notebook B' – the section of the *Notebooks* that focuses on topics that he would soon systematize in the *New Theory of Vision* – Berkeley first considers Molyneux's problem. The Irish philosopher William Molyneux had written a letter to Locke proposing a thought experiment that Locke subsequently incorporated in the second edition of his *Essay*.[23] Imagine that a man born blind can distinguish between two objects, say a sphere and a cube 'of the same metal, and nighly of the same bigness'. Further imagine he is given sight. Would the man, Molyneux asked be able to tell the sphere and cube apart just by looking at them and without touching them? If the blind man *can* know or infer which is the sphere and which is the cube by sight without touching them, then there is likely some sort of connection between the different senses, for example a common sense.[24]

Locke answered 'No' to his Irish correspondent's question: 'for though he has obtain'd the experience of, how a Globe, how a Cube affects his touch; yet he has not yet attained the Experience, that what affects his touch so or so, must affect his sight so or so' (*E* II.11, §8). Locke quickly returned to the main thread of his argument without drawing out the consequences of his position. This brief aside in the *Essay* became a touchstone in philosophy for centuries after,[25] due in no small part to how young Berkeley seized on the problem. In the *New Theory of Vision* and other writings, Berkeley developed the idea that each sense had its own distinct sense-object (*NTV* 136): the sense of touch had its 'minima tangibile', and the sense of sight its 'minima visibile' – neither of which was reducible to the other. This seems strange, because we interconnect the testimony of our different senses through experience nearly from birth. Berkeley said of himself: 'I wonder not at my sagacity in discovering the obvious, tho' amazing truth, I instead wonder at my stupid inadvertancy in not finding it out before. 'tis no witchcraft to see' (*PC* 279).

Berkeley was also focused on a number of other issues in Locke's *Essay*. First, Berkeley questioned Locke's presumption that there are unknown and unperceived substances which stand beneath and support the particular sensible qualities we experience *as* the object. We will soon see that this is one of the driving arguments for Berkeley's immaterialism. Berkeley also drew on and questioned many other of Locke's distinctions: most notably, his theory of abstraction, and his distinction between ideas of primary qualities like extension and ideas of secondary qualities like colours and smells. The criticism of abstraction was central to the *Principles,* but less evident in the *Dialogues*; the distinction between primary and secondary qualities was prominent in both works. Locke used the primary/secondary quality distinction to explain how we experience a wide range of qualities while at the same time distinguishing between the explanatory and causal roles of these qualities. So I might perceive 'this patch of blue' and 'this extended thing' – in fact I might perceive the qualities in one and the same object 'this blue ball' – but differentiate between the kinds of qualities, in so far as 'blue' is caused by and explained by 'extended atoms', but not vice versa. Berkeley found these distinctions between quality, idea of quality, and types of qualities to be dubious, for reasons we will discuss when we begin analyzing the *Dialogues*.

Malebranche

As with his other influences, Berkeley took pains to distinguish his own philosophical positions from Malebranche's, and was scandalized when early reviewers and readers represented him as a knee-jerk Malebranchist.[26] Malebranche's influence on Berkeley was large though, and has been important for twentieth-century historians of philosophy because it showed that the common pedagogic distinction between 'British empiricism' and 'Continental rationalism' made for dubious history.[27] The French rationalist Malebranche had strong adherents among British philosophers such as John Norris,[28] and was translated into English many times in the late seventeenth and early eighteenth century. He continued as an influence on British philosophers well after Berkeley wrote the *Principles* and the *Dialogues*, most importantly on Hume's *A Treatise* (primarily through his occasionalism and his theory of the passions).

Malebranche was associated with two controversial doctrines: 'Vision in God' and occasionalism. Like many other seventeenth-century philosophers – Spinoza, Leibniz, Locke, Pufendorf, *et alia* – Malebranche was deeply influenced by Descartes, but rejected the close connection made by Descartes between innateness and truth, and the further strong distinction between innate ideas and other sorts of perceptions.

Malebranche used 'perception' in a very broad way that included everything mental from feelings to sense-perception to different degrees of knowledge. He drew an important distinction between two types or categories of 'perception'. I perceive that '2 + 2 = 4', for example, quite differently from how I perceive that a ball is blue. If I was given dragonfly eyesight I might properly perceive a ball to be alive with ultra-violet colours and to contain no blue at all. A change in my sensory apparatus would result in changes in how and what I perceived. Malebranche refers to these as perception 'in the soul', and the category includes many of our modes of thought. But we also perceive things outside the soul. We perceive material bodies (which I will consider in a moment). And we perceive objective truths such as '2 + 2 = 4'. A change in my eyes or ears or nose or my brain or my soul/mind would not change that '2 + 2' equals '4', since '2 + 2 = 4' it is not just correct for me, or those like me: it is objectively true.[29] Descartes famously suggested the possibility that perhaps God might make '2 + 2' not equal '4' if he so chose,[30] and this seemed to Malebranche to be an error arising from the conflation of the criterion for recognizing that an idea is true (the transparency or clarity and distinctness of the idea), with the truth of the idea.

Descartes' conflation goes hand-in-glove with innatism, because if the idea is innate it is all the more difficult to distinguish the properties of the ideas that tell us the idea is true from the content[31] of the idea. Given all of this, Malebranche thought that we should divide our perceptions into two types: those that are peculiar to a particular mind or soul, and those that hold objectively. The former are specific to particular minds and bodies (dragonfly or human), while the latter perceptions are of ideas, external to our particular minds and bodies and representing true states of affairs that our minds have as their objects. It seemed clear to Malebranche that many of the perceptions that Descartes took to be knowledge of innate ideas in our mind or soul – ideas of mathematicals for example – were in fact perceptions of ideas outside of our minds.

What about the relation between the ways we perceive truth and how God does? One possibility is that our 'minds do not see the same, but similar truths . . . God sees that two times two are four. You see it, I see it. Here are three similar truths, not a single and unique truth.' In the 'Dialogues on Metaphysics and Religion', Malebranche's mouthpiece Aristes responds:

There are three similar perceptions of one and the same truth, but how are these three similar truths? And who told you they are similar? Have you compared your ideas with mine and with those of God, so as to recognize the resemblance clearly? Who told you that tomorrow, that through all the centuries, you will see as you do today that two times two are four? Who told you that even God cannot make minds capable of seeing two times two are not four? Surely it is because you see the same truth that I see, but by a perception which is not mine, though perhaps similar to mine . . . Now, if your ideas are eternal and immutable, it is evident that they can be found only in the eternal and immutable substance of divinity . . . It is in God alone that we see the truth.[32]

The identification of 'objective', 'external to our minds', and 'archetypal' is old and hallowed. According to this identification, to know a triangle is to access the form of the triangle or an archetypical triangle. Those ideas that we do perceive objectively are, according to

Malebranche, the actual archetypes on the basis of which God created the world. You might of course ask: why does God need archetypes? One answer might be that in order for God to choose, and consequently for there to be some contingency in the world, God must decide between different possible models, plans or archetypes. There was a tradition, associated with Platonists, which took knowing some thing as accessing the form or archetype of that thing. In a theist philosophy (in particular a Christian, Jewish or Muslim philosophy), to know the form of something was to access a form that God created and knew in order to create. Malebranche was presenting a modern, i.e. post-Cartesian, variant on these sorts of theories; and Berkeley had many philosophical affinities with these theories as well.

So far so good for ideas like our ideas of triangles. But, in the case of our perceptions of extended bodies, how can we be sure that external bodies really correspond to the ideas we take as representing them? How can we know there really are such bodies? In the *Meditations* Descartes argued that since we know that God is *not* a deceiver, we can know for certain that he would not systematically deceive us about these important facts once they had undergone a rational reflection. The 'rational reflection' proviso is essential, because our perception involves systematic deception all the time.

Malebranche thought that Descartes overstated the case, and that at best we could have probable knowledge or moral certitude of the existence of bodies, not 'geometrical' certitude. Malebranche claimed, *contra* Descartes, that 'when we perceive bodies, let us judge only that we perceive them and that these perceptible or intelligible bodies exist; but why should we judge positively that there is an external material world like the intelligible world we perceive.'[33] This did not lead Malebranche, however, to advocate immaterialism. Rather he argued that the preponderance of evidence favours our natural dispositions to believe in the existence of bodies, as does the testimony of Scripture. But we must be content with the fact that we will never know with geometrical certainty whether there are bodies beyond our ideas.

One can easily imagine Berkeley reading this discussion with great interest and wondering whether Malebranche was really correct and the probable evidence did really weigh on the side of the existence of a material world. Or was there some sort of solution to the sceptical doubt that avoided positing an external, unthinking and unthought world of extension? Berkeley wrote in his *Notebooks*:

> Malbranch in his Illustration differs widely from me He doubts of the existence of Bodies I doubt not the least of this. I differ from the Cartesians in that I make extension, Colour etc to exist really in Bodies & independent of Our Mind. All ys carefully and lucidly to be set forth. (*PC* 800–1)

He thought that Cartesian certitude built on Cartesian scepticism led to Malebranche's doubts, and that immaterialism was emetic and cure. The problem was how to salvage the existence of mind independent[34] bodies without positing the existence of matter.

Malebranche's occasionalism was also important for Berkeley. Malebranche broadly accepted Cartesian physics, with a few notable divergences.[35] Cartesian physics identified extension and bodies, and took the physical world as made up of passive extended bodies that needed some other active force to bring them into motion. Malebranche argued that, try as you might, you will not find anything in or about bodies themselves that is able to fully explain their interactions.[36] At the same time he did not want to posit an active force in the matter itself, because this tended towards materialism – 'the most dangerous error of the philosophy of the ancients'[37] – in allowing material bodies to cause and to move without the concurrence of a mind. Malebranche's solution was, instead, that God was the mover and the various concurrences of bodies only provided the occasion.

Now let's see how Berkeley synthesized and responded to his influences in dialogue form.

CHAPTER TWO

OVERVIEW OF THEMES

Berkeley belonged to an important if comparatively underdiscussed generation of British philosophers. Philosophers of the previous generation wrote at the conclusion of the turmoil of the seventeenth century, when the conflict and religious upheaval was beginning to wind down as various solutions – the Westphalian peace, the Glorious Revolution and accession of the Orange monarchs William and Mary to the British throne, the end of the religious strife fragmenting the Dutch Republic, and more horrifically the Revocation of the Edict of Nantes and the mass exodus of Protestants from France. All brought shifts in populations and attitudes throughout Europe. Philosophers like Locke, Hobbes, Spinoza, Descartes, and Malebranche all lived amid these conflicts and responded to them, as well as theorized them, from many perspectives. Some philosophers argued for moral and political solutions through strong states, others for a removal from the conflicted world of thuggish and ignorant people.

Berkeley's successors, Hume, Smith, Rousseau, Kant and the most familiar figures of eighteenth-century philosophy all wrote in the final two-thirds of the eighteenth century. In between are many less known but still very important philosophers, stretching from Shaftesbury, Bayle and Samuel Clarke, through Hutcheson, Joseph Butler, and Berkeley. All of these men were deeply concerned with the relation between morality, religion, and knowledge. Moral philosophy is least apparent in Berkeley of all of these philosophers, but this is in part due to the fact that we tend to wish to read him as concerned with philosophical issues that can be bracketed from his religious interests, and we rarely read those of his works that are directly concerned with moral philosophy: 'Passive Obedience' and *Alciphron*. It also has to do with more recent history: the fact that A.J. Ayer and others who developed Berkeley-inspired sense datum theories were thoroughly disapproving of religion and nearly as disapproving of much of what passed for morals. Ayer argued for a Berkeley without God, but he might just as well have argued for a Berkeley without morals (and did in fact, by extension).

All of which is a long way of saying that the central theme that threads through the *Three Dialogues* is immaterialism, and Berkeley's argument that matter does not exist, but that this should be understood as a pressing question for our moral and religious welfare. When Hylas first encounters Philonous in the garden he presumes that Philonous is avowing immaterialism as a controversial sceptical position in much the way someone in a college class will always declare him or herself a nihilist or a moral relativist to spark debate. But it soon becomes apparent that Philonous is willing to argue for immaterialism in earnest and not because it is a controversial doctrine. Berkeley enjoyed ideas that shocked, but he also would as soon have avowed a non-controversial position if he thought it true, and in fact he goes to great lengths to argue that immaterialism ought to be non-controversial (even if it is in fact controversial).

The dialogue form has many advantages for Berkeley, not least because it allowed him to offer immaterialism as promoting a virtuous way of life through the character of Philonous. Plato's dialogues centered around the life of Socrates, and Plato offered him as a complicated but morally virtuous ideal, even if (and when) they discussed topics far afield from morals. This was also a popular way of understanding dialogues in the Renaissance (most notably Nicolas of Cusa's *Of Learned Ignorance*) and the early modern period. Of the hurtful criticisms in Percival's letter reporting the reception of the *Principles*, the accusation that seemed to bother Berkeley the most was that he was just presenting immaterialism in order to shock, and that he couldn't possibly be seriously entertaining it. In Philonous we have a temperate and devout exponent of Berkeley's position whose serious commitment to immaterialism is unquestionable within the narrative structure of the dialogue. The discussions are civil and thoughtful. Countless objections are seriously entertained and responded to with care. In Philonous we have both the opposite of a philosopher who seeks to shock for its own sake, and an idealized picture of Berkeley.

The central points Berkeley wishes to make in the *Three Dialogues* are that matter does not exist; that all that we perceive are ideas; and that acceptance of this picture is consistent with – indeed promoting of – proper belief in God and a moral outlook. In other words, if through careful and deliberative reasoning you come to the conclusion that matter does not exist and that all we perceive are ideas, this will reinforce your belief in God in a way that will lead to a happy, composed, believing, and decent life. There is an important point for reading Berkeley lurking here. When we read a philosopher like Berkeley we tend to ask: What sorts of justifications for his positions are available without recourse to God? We think this for a good reason: his arguments for God are highly questionable, in particular after the appearance of the next great British dialogue – Hume's *Dialogues concerning Natural Religion*. But, for Berkeley, that we would have arguments *without* God would be a disaster. It would push God out of the picture in a way directly opposed to Berkeley's larger philosophical purpose.

Immaterialism is a strange doctrine to most, and there is much labour in the *Three Dialogues* devoted to showing us that it is less strange upon examination than on first blush. To grasp some of Berkeley's intuitions about matter, consider two quick, characteristically Berkeleyan arguments. First, we know of matter through our acquaintance with the world and through scientific experiments, but we are only acquainted with the world and scientific experiments through our perceptions. So we only know matter through perceptions. But then what we have immediate acquaintance with is always perceptions, not matter. Second, what scientific experiments do tell us about matter is continuously changing, as cyclotrons get larger and experimental apparatus more sophisticated. Each substantial category we acquire that reflects observations seems quickly to be shown to be highly questionable as a substantive. Matter becomes atoms, becomes protons and neutrons, becomes quarks, and perhaps becomes strings. But what are these? We do not know whether light is a wave or a particle. Abstractions based on experimental knowledge are mediated by perception. And the further we plumb into the 'essence' of matter, the further we seem to travel from an underlying subject we predicate, stuff that has colours and shapes and sizes. These claims are by no means decisive. But they are intuitive enough, and a reason not to reject Berkeley's position without first thinking it through.

Immaterialism is tied up with idealism for Berkeley to the point that he tends to take them as correlative. However, they need not be correlative: in fact, Berkeley tenders an objection in the 'Second

Dialogue' that there could be something other than matter and ideas – so one might hold that there are ideas, and something else, but that this something else is not matter. Since Berkeley 'idealism' has come to mean many things, and the word is most notably associated with German idealism. There were also British Idealists, American Idealists, and of course Platonic Idealists (for whom Berkeley had sympathy). Berkeley holds idealism and immaterialism as correlative because of another -ism: empiricism. If empiricism is the doctrine that all we know and we perceive, we know through the senses, by reflection, or by both, then Berkeley will seek to show that from this it follows that all we know are our perceptions and reflections on our perceptions. Then all we know or have acquaintance with are our ideas (in the broad sense). Matter is not supposed to be made of ideas.

How are these issues presented in the *Three Dialogues*? The 'First Dialogue' is divided into four main parts. In the opening section, Berkeley sets the scene and defines scepticism and the important distinction between mediate and immediate perception. In the second part, Berkeley considers qualities perceived by the senses that appear to be peculiarly dependent on the perceiver, such as perceptions of colour, heat and cold, sounds, etc. In the third part, Berkeley investigates our ideas of qualities that appear to be independent, such as solidity and extension. In the final part, he begins to attack Locke's doctrine of representation and to develop his immaterialism. This includes both the famous 'Master Argument' and his criticisms of Locke's doctrines of resemblance.

The 'Second Dialogue' is the briefest of the three dialogues, but pivotal. Like any good trilogy, act two of three must move us from somewhere to somewhere, but must have intrinsic interest as well. Some of the intermediate sections of great works of philosophy are their zeniths: Aristotle's *Metaphysics* 7–10 and the middle books of the *Republic* are two examples. Other great works of philosophy seem to lag somewhere in the middle.

In the 'Second Dialogue' Berkeley briskly treats two main topics, and there's little time for tedium. After briefly ruling out the brain as the cause of sense perceptions, Philonous provides an interesting proof of God as following from his account of perception. Then Hylas tries to save the existence of matter through offering different ways in which matter might serve as an intermediate cause or an occasion. This leads him to a discussion of Malebranche's philosophy. Philonous shows that none of Hylas' proposed avenues evade the criticisms established in the 'First Dialogue'.

The 'Third Dialogue' treats a wide variety of themes, ranging from how we know that 'snow is white', to the doctrine of notions, to an account of action, to an immaterialist account of the Mosaic creation. It is a bit of a hodgepodge, rounding up loose objections. But it also includes some of Berkeley's most intriguing, if inconclusive notions. And it makes clear that the work is very much about spirits: ours and others, and God.

CHAPTER THREE

READING THE TEXT

'PREFACE' AND THE 'FIRST DIALOGUE' (II: 167–207)

The commentary on the 'First Dialogue' is *far* longer than the comment on the two dialogues which follow it. This is mostly due to the greater need for conceptual and historical stage-setting: much more needs to be said about Berkeley's initial concepts and arguments at the beginning than when they are referred back to later. And some concepts need to be treated, notably abstraction, which Berkeley only discusses scantily. The 'First Dialogue' also includes most of Berkeley's best-known arguments and ideas. It is preceded by a brief, but important, preface to the work as a whole.

The Preface (167–9)

Berkeley opens the *Three Dialogues* with a common theme of late seventeenth and early eighteenth century British philosophy, by stating that the ultimate goal of speculation is moral improvement – the 'improvement or regulation of our lives and actions'. Similar themes are voiced in the works of Berkeley's contemporaries and immediate predecessors. For instance, in the 'Introduction' to the *Essay concerning Human Understanding*, John Locke stressed that the purpose of knowledge was not to plumb the mysteries of the universe but rather to know 'whatsoever is necessary for the Conveniences of Life, and the Information of Virtue' (*E* I.1.5). Locke initially undertook writing the *Essay* to settle disputes among his friends on morality and religion, and throughout the *Essay* he cautioned his readers not to sail into the 'vast Ocean of Being', and not to attempt to 'know all things, but those which concern our Conduct' (*E* I.1.6). This sentiment was shared by Berkeley and was essential to the larger project. Berkeley thought that although Locke and others expressed these goals as integral to their works, they still allowed themselves to be misled by erroneous and wilful speculation, away from the common world. Despite themselves, their doctrines bred *scepticism*.

'Scepticism' had at least as many meanings in the seventeenth and early eighteenth century as it does today. Sometimes it signified the ancient doctrines associated with Sextus Empiricus, Pyrrho and the Academic Sceptics; sometimes it just meant non-dogmatic inquiry associated with the new science and the Royal Society (Robert Boyle's *Sceptical Chymist,* for example, or Joseph Glanvill's *The Vanity of Dogmatizing*); and sometimes it was a synonym for irreligion and immoralism. In fact, the vagueness of the signification of the word 'scepticism' is important for Berkeley's argument, as we will soon see. When it was invoked in philosophical contexts in the early eighteenth century it was often associated with the works of Pierre Gassendi, Pierre Nicole, and above all the great Rotterdam philosopher Pierre Bayle.[1] Bayle was born in France to a Jansenist family. He converted briefly to Catholicism and then back to Protestantism, and left France along with nearly the entire Protestant population when the Edict of Nantes (which had tolerated non-Catholics) was revoked in 1685 by Louis XIV. Needless to say, Bayle had a visceral understanding of how even the most powerful beliefs could be poorly founded. His widely read work, the *Historical and Philosophical Dictionary,* included a famous article on the ancient sceptic Pyrrho, which was a touchstone for many early eighteenth-century discussions of scepticism.

In the article 'Pyrrho', Bayle defined Pyrrhonism (which was synonymous with scepticism for many readers) as 'the art of disputing about all things and always suspending one's judgment'. Opponents of scepticism characterized the position as embracing contradictions or paradoxes, but this was a misconstrual. Rather, sceptics showed that either of two contradictory positions could be argued for equally rationally, and consequently that adopting one or the other position was dogmatic. By undermining dogmas and by accepting that in most cases the reasons for holding any position are sufficiently underdetermined that the opposite can also be maintained with valid supporting reasons, the sceptic suspended judgment and attained a state of agnostic tranquility (*not* a dogmatic embrace of paradox).

Bayle thought that this anti-dogmatism was consistent with science and public morals but posed a serious threat to religion. Science benefited from continuous challenge to dogma, and some of the most important figures of early modern scientific inquiry – like Gassendi and Hobbes – combined sceptical methodology and Epicurian atomistic explanation. Bayle, and later Hume, argued that scepticism rarely if ever seems to undermine moral conduct, and that in fact sceptics often tend to lead morally blameless lives. This was a pervasive theme in early modern philosophy, from Grotius' notorious claim that civil society could exist without religion, to Hobbes' attempt to put civil society on an artificial footing, to Bayle's claims that an atheist could be perfectly moral.

As mentioned above, Europe of the later sixteenth and the seventeenth century was packed with religious violence: the aforementioned Civil Wars in France, the Thirty Years War, the English Civil War, and the Glorious Revolution. Many late seventeenth-century philosophers responded to these conflicts with moral and political theories that attempted to diminish conflict by putting religious and political control in the hands of a sole arbitrator (Hobbes), or splitting religious and confessional roles (the influential natural lawyer Samuel Pufendorf or, in a very different way, Locke), or developing a minimal, shared, natural religion that was not susceptible to conflict (Grotius, Leibniz, and in a very different way Locke). There was also a sceptical response best expressed by Bayle, who recognized that beliefs of many sorts cannot be dislodged by reason or (often) violence, and suspending judgment is appropriate if possible.

By the time that Berkeley was writing, the Glorious Revolution was 20 years in the past and England was comparatively stable. But the question of how morals, political order, and religion were connected was still central. If one viewed public morals, as Berkeley and many others did, as connected to (broadly) religious justifications (such as final judgment in the afterlife or divine providence), then the sceptic's stress on the independence of morals from religious belief becomes more dubious,[2] and the pressure exerted on religion from scepticism becomes not only impious but also immoral (and Berkeley would add politically destructive as well).

An example of how these concerns were connected for Berkeley can be seen by briefly considering the doctrine seen by Bayle as the first consequence of Pyrrho's art: that 'the absolute and internal nature of objects is hidden from us and that we can only be sure of how they appear to us in various respects.' This doctrine was central to sceptics and one of Sextus' basic principles: 'honey appears to us to be sweet (and this we grant, for we perceive sweetness through the senses), but whether it is also sweet in its essence is for us a matter of doubt, since this is not an appearance but a judgment regarding the appearance.'[3] This was a recurrent theme in eighteenth-century philosophy, from Locke's distinction between a nominal essence which we can access and a real essence which is beyond our access in Book III of the *Essay*, to Kant's famous claims about the 'thing in itself'.

In the 'Preface' to the *Three Dialogues*, Berkeley identified the per- ceived gulf between 'the existence of things' and what is 'perceived', and the 'real nature' of things and 'that which falls under our senses' as the sources of scepticism. Twenty years later in *Alciphron*, Berkeley had the irreligious, sceptical Alciphron say: 'Know then, that the shallow Mind of the Vulgar, as it dwells only on the outward Surface of things, and considers them in the gross, may be easily imposed on. Hence a blind Reverence for religious Faith' (*A* VII.1). In other words, the distinction between surface knowledge and deep essential knowledge can be used by sceptical atheists to undermine the 'surface' phenomenon of religious faith and belief by referring to hidden causes that we cannot access, and whose existence under- mines the independent validity of faith and other 'surface'.

In addition, the search for depth tends to enervate and distract modern philosophers. 'Vain speculation' leads men away from their true duties and purposes and to irreligion. Berkeley's goal was:

> In order, therefore, to divert the busy mind of man from vain researches . . . to inquire into the source of its perplexities; and, if possible, to lay down such principles, as, by an easy solution of them, together with their own native evidence, may at once rec- ommend themselves for genuine to the mind, and rescue it from the endless pursuits it is engaged in. Which, with a plain demon- stration of the immediate Providence of an all-seeing God, and the natural immortality of the soul, should seem the readiest preparation, as well as the strongest motive, to the study and practice of virtue. (*D* II: 167)

Given all of this, Berkeley's own avowedly anti-sceptical position is closer to that of Sextus and the Hellenistic sceptics than to irreli- gious modern dogmatists – to embrace surfaces and not worry about essences. This kinship is something that Hume no doubt noticed in Berkeley's arguments. But for Berkeley it was a push to limit inquiry to its appropriate bounds. He stated the point elegantly in the 'Introduction' to the *Principles*:

> In vain do we extend our view into the heavens, and pry into the entrails of the earth, in vain do we consult the writings of learned men, and trace the dark footsteps of antiquity; we need only draw the curtain of words, to behold the fairest tree of knowledge, whose fruit is excellent, and within the reach of our hand. (P 'Introduction,' § 24)

Unfortunately the curtain of words is crusted over with a long history of the erroneous use of terms and has grown musty and stiff. It is also a mark of human hubris that we take our derivative words to be more important than God's words – God's visual language, which Philonous admires in the garden. But unfortunately the curtain is not so simple to draw!

The Setting (171–2)

The 'First Dialogue' opens with a chance encounter between the two characters whose conversations are the substance of each of the three dialogues: Philonous and Hylas. It was common practice from the Renaissance onward to give characters in philosophical dialogues names derived from Greek and Latin words that told the reader something about them (as opposed to how Plato used the names of real historical figures like Socrates and Alcibiades in his dialogues). 'Philonous' means 'lover of the mind' or 'lover of knowledge' (which is an appropriate epithet for Berkeley as well, as we shall see) in Greek. He functions as Berkeley's spokesman throughout the *Three Dialogues,* and appropriately speaks first (he also has the final word of the 'Third Dialogue').[4] The very first words of the dialogue are Philonous' greeting: 'Good morrow, Hylas: I did not expect to find you abroad so early' (*D* II:171). 'Hylas' is the Greek word for matter. The character 'Hylas' is a stand-in for the modern philosophy, associated with Locke and many others, which Berkeley thought of as a materialist breeding-ground for scepticism and irreligion. At the same time, Hylas and Philonous are civil and even friendly throughout. Berkeley thought of the philosophy of Locke and others as less malicious than misguided and in need of a 'revolt from metaphysical notions to the plain dictates of Nature and common sense' (*D* II: 172).

As with Plato's *Republic* and *Symposium*, the opening and closing of all three of Berkeley's *Dialogues* contain literary details that provide context for the arguments to follow. Philonous begins the dialogue by noting that Hylas is up uncharacteristically early. This greeting implies that Hylas is the sort of person who stays up late and rarely wakes early: one who is likely not leading the most proper life. As it turns out, Hylas is awake so early because he has never slept: he has stayed up all night due to philosophical agitation!

Setting the dialogue in the early morning in a garden might have brought Bernard Bouvier de Fontenelle's[5] extremely popular 'Conversations on the Plurality of Worlds' to mind for his readers. The 'Conversations' was first published in 1686 but continued to be influential throughout the eighteenth century. In the work, a philosopher and a beautiful Marquise sit in a garden – the natural home of the Epicurean sect – and flirt, stare at the night sky and playfully speculate on life on other planets in a mechanistic and Epicurean universe.[6] They both accept that lying behind our perceptions are mechanistically governed concations of atoms, and indeed delight in it.[7] Philosophizing at night, as opposed to by the morning light, opens the mind to French licence, Epicureanism, and atheism!

In the opening of the *Three Dialogues*. Berkeley intimates that Hylas is out of touch with the beauty and wonder of sense experience (as opposed to sensual experience!), knowledge of which is 'within the reach of our hand', and that his preference for the darkness of night and comparative lack of sense experience is fodder for unmoored metaphysical speculation. Philonous follows Hylas' confession that he has been up all night by describing the sensual beauty of the garden where they now speak in the early morning: the purple sky of sunrise, bird songs, and the smells of trees and flowers. Philonous adds that 'the faculties too being at this time fresh and lively, are fit for those meditations, which the solitude of a garden and tranquility of the morning naturally disposes us to.' For the Berkeleyan philosopher there is no conflict between sensible delight and meditation. He does not seek to shut out the world of the senses but rather attend to what the senses really tell us – 'purple', 'gentle', 'delightful', and so forth – and what they ultimately indicate or point towards.

This seems in studied opposition to the opening of Malebranche's *Dialogue on Metaphysics and Religion* as well. The *Dialogue on Metaphysics* opens with Malebranche's mouthpiece, Theodore, suggesting that he and Aristes retire to his study where they will better be able to discuss philosophy and consult sovereign Reason undisturbed by the senses. Aristes remarks: 'I am disgusted with everything I see in this material and sensible world,' and Theodore replies: 'I shall teach you that the word that you live in is not as you believe it to be, because actually it is not the way you see or sense it.'[8] The sceptical consequences of philosophizing in the 'closet' or study away from the common world is a recurrent theme in British philosophy, made famous in Hume's 'sceptical' conclusion to Book I of *A Treatise*. Speculation in the 'closet' *à la* Malebranche has none of the natural limits offered by the company of non-philosophers and the world of ordinary things, and thus breeds fanciful metaphysical doctrines that are only a step removed from the atheism and Epicureanism of Fontenelle. It might be harmless in and of itself to speculate on wild and untenable metaphysical notions, but when it is promoted as the seductive pastime of men and women of leisure, 'men of less leisure will be tempted to entertain Suspicions concerning the most important Truths, which they had hitherto held sacred and unquestionable' (*D* II: 172).

It might seem strange to us that Berkeley would believe that misguided philosophical speculation could result in the breakdown of social order, but as I noted in the previous section this was a commonplace idea at the time when he was writing. In between the publication of the *Principles* and the *Dialogues*, Berkeley gave three sermons, which were then published in 1712 as a pamphlet entitled 'Passive Obedience'.[9] In this pamphlet he argued for a close connection between moral order, civil order, and religious hierarchy. In Berkeley's view, our duties to other human beings are put in place by God in order to tend towards the general well-being of men. Duties and rules may or may not educe to the benefit of a particular man or woman, but the system as a whole is for the well-being of all men. To violate a duty towards a particular man, or to break a civil law, is to undermine the general good for which the system was created, and to attack God as the establisher of the system. For truth, moral and religious decency, and social order it is best to philosophize in the daylight!

What kept Hylas up all night in philosophical agitation? The evening before Hylas had heard Philonous' philosophy represented as wilfully undermining common sense with a wild, sceptical and paradoxical doctrine, namely that 'there is no such thing as material substance in the world' (*D* II: 172). To Hylas' surprise, Philonous embraces the characterization of his position, and much of the rest of the *Three Dialogues* is spent defending it and showing that it is fully in line with common sense, as well as with responsible morality, religion, philosophy, mathematics, and natural science.

Indeed, according to Philonous, the rejection of matter is not just the denial of a falsehood, but a liberation, a 'Revolt from Metaphysical Notions to the plain Dictates of Nature and *common Sense*' (my emphasis – AG). He remarks further: 'I find my Understanding strangely enlightened, so that I can now easily comprehend a great many Things which before were all Mystery and Riddle.' In characterizing his philosophy, Berkeley uses the phrase 'common sense' in a novel and influential manner. For many philosophers who wrote before Berkeley, 'common sense' or 'sensus communis' referred to power of the imagination, which unified different kinds of sense experience. It began to gain a different sense for philosophers in the late seventeenth and early eighteenth century. Shaftesbury was crucial in this change. One of the sections of Shaftesbury's *Characteristicks* is entitled 'Sensus Communis: An Essay on the Freedom of Wit and Humor', and he uses 'common sense' there to mean: 1. the 'Sense of Publick Good, and the common Interest of Mankind;'[10] 2. minimal rational capacity;[11] 3. beliefs shared by all men and women; 4. first, untutored thoughts in opposition to refined sense. Of these, number 4 is particularly important for Berkeley, and the following passage from Shaftesbury uses 'common sense' in a way fully consonant with the passage from Berkeley's *Dialogues* I just quoted:

> In the main, 'tis best to stick to *Common Sense*, and go no further. Mens first Thoughts, in this matter, are generally better than their second: their natural Notions better than those refin'd by Study, or Consulation with *Casuists*. According to common Speech, as well as common Sense, *Honesty is the best Policy*: But according to refin'd Sense, the only *well–advis'd* Persons, as to this World, are *errant Knaves*; and they alone are thought to serve themselves, who serve their Passions, and indulge their loosest Appetites and Desires. _ Such, it seems, are *the Wise*, and such *the Wisdom of this World*![12]

After Berkeley, 'common sense' became associated with the Scottish 'common sense' philosophers Thomas Reid, James Beattie, and James Oswald, and with the Berkeleyan idea that philosophers of a metaphysical bent wilfully obscure basic principles which ordinary people immediately assent to upon rational reflection and which ought to be the core of proper philosophy. We might think that the existence of matter is an evident principle, but Philonous will try to show that this is not the case. When an ordinary person sees a frog on a table do they say to themselves, 'A ha! Matter!', or rather 'Look! A frog on a table!'?

But what can stand as a test for whether a doctrine qualifies as a common sense, plain dictate of nature? Self-evidence might be a possible criterion, but given that so many of our common sense beliefs are crusted over with questionable metaphysical doctrines. how can we be sure that a given doctrine is self-evident? Hylas considers the existence of matter as one of the 'plainest Things in Nature', so a way of adjucating between competing principles claiming to be commonsensical is needed.

Philonous offers a criterion based on the consequences of holding a particular principle. Given a choice between two contrary philosophical doctrines, one should reject that doctrine which leads to more 'Paradoxes and Repugnances.' We can presume that Berkeley understands 'paradoxes and repugnances' to be doctrines that entail contradictions, since Hylas illustrates 'the part is greater than the whole' as a paradigmatically repugnant doctrine (although according to him, less repugnant than immaterialism). This gives a reasonably clear criterion[13] for adjucating between competing doctrines. To embrace a doctrine that results in greater paradox would clearly indicate scepticism and a rejection of common sense.

Defining Scepticism (172–3)

But what is scepticism? We have already discussed some of the ways in which it was understood when the *Three Dialogues* appeared, and noted that Berkeley's own position has a surprising affinity with classical Pyrrhonianism. Unsurprisingly, Berkeley sets out to define scepticism in such a way as to distance it from his own position. To this end, Berkeley moves dialectically through a series of possible definitions of scepticism offered by Hylas in order to arrive at a true definition.

Definition 1: *A sceptic is 'one that doubts of every Thing'. Conversely one 'who entertains no Doubt' on a particular point is not a sceptic with regard to that point*
This provides both a global and a local definition of the sceptic. One can be wholly a sceptic as well as a sceptic on a particular point. The definition hangs on doubting: but what is doubting? Is it affirmation, negation, or suspension of judgment? For example, I could claim to doubt that the external world exists in at least two different senses. If someone affirms that the external world exists I could negate their affirmation and affirm the positive – 'The external world does not exist.' Or, alternately, I could refuse to affirm anything at all and suspend my judgment. Classical Pyrrhonism involves both negation and suspension. To deny the existence of matter, as Philonous does, only involves the first step, and so is not sceptical by this standard. Consequently, Hylas must further qualify his definition.

Definition 2: *In addition, a sceptic is one 'who denies the Reality and Truth of Things'*
Philonous immediately asks Hylas to specify which things, since 'scientific principles are universal intellectual Notions, and consequently independent of Matter.' Hylas grants that 'scientific principles' are independent of matter with surprisingly little argument. Why does Berkeley view this as so unproblematic for his opponents? Couldn't a thorough-going materialist say that there are no 'universal intellectual notions' independent of matter? Perhaps: but Berkeley's opponent is not a thorough-going materialist, but rather an ordinary Lockean or Cartesian. It is a very important point for Berkeley. First, it establishes that there can be rational agreement between Hylas and Philonous independent of whether there is matter. Second, it shows that the disagreement between Berkeley and Lockeans and Cartesians is not a disagreement about reason as such, or reality or truth, but a more local dispute – albeit with great ramifications. This leads to a further specification of 'scepticism' that shows what is really at stake for Hylas, and that Berkeley's position is not sceptical in an ordinary sense.

Definition 3: *The greater sceptic 'denies the Reality of Sensible Things, or professes the greatest Ignorance of them'*
Berkeley's move from Definition 2 to Definition 3 is not trivial. He could have had Definition 3 assert that the sceptic 'denies the reality

of the external world' or 'denies the existence of matter'. But instead, it states that the sceptic denies or professes ignorance of the 'Reality of Sensible Things'. In order to clarify, he has Philonous ask what he understands by 'sensible things', and Berkeley has Hylas respond: 'Those Things which are perceived by the Senses.' 'The Reality of Sensible Things' in Definition 3 thus means 'the reality of objects perceived by the senses'. In this way Berkeley changes the focus of discussion from external objects or things to the mode by which we access them – sense perception.

Since Berkeley's argument is against the new philosophers, and primarily against followers of Locke, this is not as controversial an assumption as it appears, and Lockeans would likely have accepted this elision. But, as a philosophical assumption independent of this context, it is not so clear. Take for example the famous and extraordinarily clever paper from 1905 where Einstein showed that we can know that molecules made up of atoms exist, even though they are too small for us to perceive with our senses. In the nineteenth century, Robert Brown observed that pollen grains jerk around in a random manner when suspended in a liquid. Einstein showed that this can be explained by the impacts of atoms that are too small to be perceived. Furthermore, the path of the motion of the pollen grains can be predicted statistically on the basis of this hypothesis. Atoms are precisely the sorts of objects that a Lockean empiricist like Hylas would hold that it would be absurd to deny.

Berkeley's response will be to say that at some point knowledge depends on testimony of the senses, and then it is incumbent on us to explain how the immediate perceptual knowledge ('these pollen grains are whirling about') and the remote perceptual knowledge ('molecules and atoms') are connected. So in the Brownian motion example, we know of the atoms *through* observation of the pollen grains. In the 'Second Dialogue' Berkeley claimed:

> That from a Cause, Effect, Operation, Sign, or other Circumstance, there may reasonably be inferred the Existence of a Thing not immediately perceived, and that it were absurd for any Man to argue against the Existence of that Thing, from his having no direct and positive Notion of it, I freely own.

To this end, Berkeley introduces an account of signification via the distinction between mediate and immediate signs.

Signs and qualities (174–5)
Philonous offers an intriguing example to motivate the distinction between immediate and mediate perceptions:

> In reading a book, what I immediately perceive are the letters, but mediately, or by means of these, are suggested to my mind the notions of God, virtue, truth, &c.

Berkeley's goals in introducing the distinction between immediate and mediate perception were: first, to argue that all sense perception is immediate; second, to show that the thoughts that are mediately suggested by sense perception are not perceived by the senses; and third, to suggest an analogy between sense perception and how words signify. This last is mostly implicit in the *Dialogues* rather than explicit, but I think it is an important premise in many of Berkeley's arguments. I will discuss his account of language in later sections, but for the moment we should keep a further distinction in mind.

Early modern philosophers often distinguished between natural signs and artificial, arbitrary, or imposed signs. A sign is arbitrary or artificial when the signification does not depend on any pre-existent resemblance or connection with the signified. For example, the word 'triangle' is an arbitrary signifier for a triangle, in that any other group of letters (such as 'HUIW' or 'llyx') might in principle equally well stand for the shape; or red in a traffic light stands for 'STOP', but it is an arbitrary signifier in that it could just as easily be blue. Of course, the capacity to signify depends on prior relations: if you made all the red lights blue it would be a disaster. But these are arbitrary as well – a convention established for communication.[14]

Natural signification is a bit more confusing. Eleven years after Berkeley's death, Thomas Reid distinguished three senses in which signs can be said to be *natural*: 1. 'those whose connection with the thing signified is established by nature, but discovered by experience' (Brownian motion signifying atomic motion); 2. 'that wherein the connection between sign and thing signified, is not only established by nature, but discovered to us by a natural principle' (a causal relation for example); and 3. 'those which, though we never before had any notion or conceptions of things signified, do suggest it, or conjure it up, as it were, by a natural kind of magic, and at once give us a conception, and create a belief of it' (such as a natural belief in God, or a fear of spiders).[15]

In the *New Theory of Vision*, Berkeley offers the following example of a sign that many of his philosophical contemporaries would have taken to be a paradigmatic natural sign in all three of Reid's senses:

It is evident that when the mind perceives any idea immediately and of it self, it must be by means of some other idea. Thus for instance, the passions which are in the mind of another are of themselves to me invisible. I may nevertheless perceive them by sight, though not immediately, yet by Means of the colours they produce in the countenance. (*NTV* §9)

In this example the sign – blushing – seems to be naturally connected to the shame that it signifies. Later in the *New Theory of Vision,* Berkeley remarks:

Those passions are themselves invisible, they are nevertheless let in the eye along with colours and alterations of countenance, which are the immediate objects of vision: And which signify them *for no other reason than barely* because they have been observed to accompany them. Without which experience we should have no more taken blushing for a sign of shame than of gladness. (my emphasis: *NTV* §65)

What might seem to be a natural sign in senses 2 and 3 is, according to Berkeley, not even a natural sign in sense 1, insofar as he seems to be ruling out a natural connection established prior to our association of blushing and shame discovered through observation. If this seems a bit implausible, remember that some people turn red when not feeling shame, and others feel shame but do not blush. Furthermore, although the only way we can know such a connection is through experience, we do not ever immediately access the emotions of the person we observe blushing. It is a keystone of the general Berkeleyan project of showing people that what they often take to be 'natural' – the existence of matter – is not wholly natural, or indeed natural at all.

What hangs on the distinction between natural and artificial signification? As we will see in what follows, a great deal. One less than obvious thing (for us) is that Berkeley thought that theories that stressed natural causes, connections, and signs have little place for

God – 'to what purpose might not fate or nature serve as well as Deity, on such a scheme?' (*NTVV* §4). God can be written out of the scheme and nature can take his place, as Spinoza and his followers (*PC* 824–6) might have wished. Signification depends on a connection or relation between sign and signified, and a sign is natural according to Reid's taxonomy if the sign and what is signified are *naturally* connected. The 'natural connection' may be resemblance (a bust of Julius Caesar resembles the historical figure Julius Caesar and thus stands in for him), or a causal relation (a parent causes a child to come into existence), or some other 'necessary connexion' (a group of individuals who are part of a group with a function or a purpose). Berkeley was suspicious of such putatively natural connections, as is apparent from the blushing example. Locke viewed certain kinds of ideas as natural signs of external objects, and this dispute is at the heart of Berkeley's criticisms of Locke on representation.[16] The sign and signified are both perceived, but it is apparent that the signification relation presumes that they are perceived differently: the sign (a letter, a blush) is perceived immediately, and the signified (a sound, shame) is perceived mediately, by means of and after the sign.

'Immediate perceptions' could then be construed as both an immediate sense content (the unreflective perception of the form or shape of a letter) and a sign that can be related to something else which it signifies.[17] Hylas quickly agrees with Philonous that we do not sense objects mediately perceived – such as the causes of our perceptions – but only sensible qualities and combinations of sensible qualities specific to and immediately accessible to each of the senses. Causes, and other relations between either perceived or unperceived qualities or things, are not given in these immediate, particular sense perceptions. According to Berkeley, these perceptions are relatively inert, i.e., we cannot derive causes or other relations from them in isolation. Instead they tell us 'this sea is green' and like qualities.

So far I have only discussed immediate perceptions as signs, but they are of course ideas as well. 'Idea' is one of the slipperiest words in the philosophical vocabulary, which, given the slipperiness of the philosophical vocabulary in general, is saying a lot! Malebranche and Arnauld fought over whether all ideas are mental processes that represent objects, or are mind-independent objects themselves (in the sense I discussed earlier). Both of these ways of characterizing ideas have a Cartesian patrimony. Commentators have found many different senses of 'idea' in Locke's *Essay* as well: as objects of the understanding (in the 'Third Dialogue' Philonous asserts that ideas 'denote the immediate Objects of the Understanding' (*D* II: 236) for modern philosophers), as perceptual acts, as mental entities, as images, as natural signs, and as concepts (i.e. as general and publicly accessible).[18] In this context, Berkeley is primarily interested in Locke's ideas as representative, by which he understands them as natural signs of or representatives of ideas of some being (a rock, for example), or some other idea.

Because 'idea' is such a broad, umbrella term in seventeenth- and eighteenth-century philosophy for all sorts of mental content or mental experience, there are many ambiguities in how it is used. And unfortunately, like other seventeenth- and eighteenth-century philosophers, Berkeley tends not to distinguish between many different ways of perceiving a quality or having an idea which philosophers of the twentieth and twenty-first centuries take for granted. When I read a sentence in Berkeley's *Dialogues* such as 'Hylas do you perceive heat?' it is not clear which and what sort of perceptions or ideas Philonous (or Berkeley) means. Is Philonous asking whether Hylas has and recognizes the idea which he takes to represent a general quality such as 'heat' (and perhaps draws inferences from it or makes judgements about it)? Or whether Hylas has had the particular brute psychological experience 'HOT!'? Or whether Hylas is *capable* of perceiving heat (in either of the above senses)? Or whether Hylas *seems* to perceive heat? Or whether Hylas is *thinking about* the perception of heat? Vastly different philosophical consequences follow from how we read such ambiguous lines. Berkeley does not make these distinctions in any systematic way, and in fact he tends to elide them all into 'perceiving', 'qualities', and 'ideas'.

Much of the best writing on Berkeley turns on showing, often quite rightly, how Berkeley's failures to appreciate these distinctions result in problems for his arguments (or sometimes in stronger versions of his arguments). I will refer to these distinctions when they are particularly relevant, and they should be kept in mind in general while reading Berkeley (or any other early modern philosopher). I will stress them less than many other commentators because I want mainly to consider what Berkeley thought he was doing in general in and with the *Dialogues*. That Berkeley tends to collapse them is an important fact about his philosophical views.

The crucial point about immediate perceptions for Berkeley is, I think, that immediate perceptions or ideas must be conceptually distinguished from what they are presumed to signify. This will allow Berkeley to think of claims about representation (such as 'my perception of this sensation of hardness represents a hard snowball in the world beyond my mind which has now hit me in the head'), in terms of signification, and question how natural the relation of signification is, what it means to signify, and what is really being signified.

If perception involves signification, then we might well wonder what content or meaning is given to us in immediate perception. The thesis that little could be inferred from sensible knowledge was particularly associated with Descartes. If it could be the case that the testimony of my senses was entirely wrong, that I am floating in a void and being tormented by a malevolent genius while I believe that I am sitting by my fireplace in my study, then little can be derived from my immediate sense perception beyond its particular qualitative features. It turns out for Descartes that perceptions of extension and figure have an intellectual content amenable to rational ordering via geometry. But relations between opposed qualities like hot and cold are nearly mute. There are the trickier cases of feelings of pain and pleasure, which we will soon consider and from which we do draw various inferences, but they are often faulty as well.

In the *Third Meditation*, Descartes condemned our knowledge of sensible qualities other than size, extension, shape, motion and a few others as 'materially false':

> as for all the rest, including light and colours, sounds, smells, tastes, heat and cold, and the other tactile qualities, I think of these only in a very confused and obscure way . . . the ideas which I have of heat and cold contain so little clarity and distinctness that they do not enable me to tell whether cold is merely the absence of heat or vice versa, or whether both of them are real qualities, or neither is.[19]

As noted previously, extension, shape, etc., can be easily geometrically represented (i.e., extended lines can be used to represent extended objects on a coordinate grid which can then be characterized algebraically) in a way that the qualitative properties of heat and cold and colour cannot (and hence are a better supports for explanations). But our particular experiences of taste, touch, colour, etc. testify to little beyond qualitative features they have specific to the particular sense. They give us little relational knowledge of opposed qualities, much less knowledge of their proximate causes. Locke's view on knowledge of qualities has some affinities to that of Descartes, but with far greater stress laid upon sense knowledge. Malebranche, Berkeley's other major influence, was less ambiguous in arguing that one cannot infer causes or much else from immediate sense perceptions of all sorts, and that real knowledge came from a purely intellectual intuition or perception.

We can see then that the position to which Hylas assents was held by some of Berkeley's influential opponents, either in whole or in part. Yet in spite of Hylas' quick acquiescence, it is not obvious that we do not perceive mediate objects of sense with our senses as well. Berkeley's letter example gives us immediate and mediate objects of sense, where the mediate objects are images ('letters') and the mediate objects things which seem particularly resistance to reduction images. It's even a sin to have an image of God!

Perhaps, though, there are less clear-cut cases between the extremes of letters and God. J.L. Austin cited some interesting examples which we can use to problematize the distinction between direct sense perception and indirect sense perception:

> We might contrast seeing you directly with seeing, say, your shadow on the blind; and perhaps we might contrast hearing the music directly with hearing it relayed outside the concert-hall.[20]

Or think of listening to a radio with bad reception. When you listen to the radio you seem not to be listening just to music, but to a bad radio with bad reception. These are cases of mediated perception, but they also seem to be as sense perceptions (or at least it's not obvious that they don't). The examples are intriguing because they question where, and what, indirect perception is, and they intimate that indirect sense perception is not only possible but commonplace. They also make us think about what might be the actual content of sense perception. Austin is criticizing Berkeley-inspired sense-datum theories such as that of A.J. Ayer, which held that what we ultimately perceive when we see shadows on a blind are not 'shadows' but little grey and coloured bits in a visual field that we can then describe in a variety of different ways. But it is not obvious that we don't perceive in more qualitatively and informationally rich bundles – 'bad radio', for example.

We could also criticize Berkeley's limiting of sense perception in another, related way. Maybe sense perception is a broader category than Berkeley allows, and takes in not just images but also beauty, and other complex qualities. This was a position held by Shaftesbury and later by Hutcheson (and one which Berkeley criticized in *Alciphron*), that 'sense' is much broader than the five external senses. Berkeley seems to be implicitly narrowing sense at the same time as he is distinguishing it from other kinds of thoughts in terms of its immediacy. We will have to see whether this is an accurate criticism of Berkeley.

The restriction of sense perception to the immediate perception or reception of qualities specific to each of the senses is an important initial step in Berkeley's argument that to be a sensible thing is to be perceived – that *'esse* is *percipi'* (*P* 3). This in turn is a crucial step in his argument for immaterialism, since if he can convince the reader that to be a sensible thing is *just* to be perceived by one or more senses, then sensible things only exists as perceived by the senses, i.e., as sensible qualities and groups of sensible qualities. If inaccessible bundles of atoms beneath perceptible qualities are not immediately perceived they do not exist (although then there is the serious problem of what gives bundles of ideas their unity). This is not to say that they are not possible, just that they are not actual. Conversely, to deny *'esse* is *percipi'* is to allow that there may be wholly unperceived things, qualities or object, which exist and yet are perceivable by the senses. This latter is a highly intuitively plausible position. There may be a missing shade of blue, for example, which no one has perceived, but it seems crazy to say that since it is not perceived then it is does not exist as a sense-perceivable colour. I could just say that it's the shade of blue between two shades I and others have perceived, which again seems perfectly reasonable. So the burden of proof is squarely on Berkeley!

Berkeley begins his argument by investigating how we perceive colours, sounds, heat and cold, smells, and tastes. Locke referred to all of these sense perceptions as 'ideas of secondary qualities' – a term he probably derived from his friend Robert Boyle, the great early modern experimentalist and founder of the Royal Society.[21] Locke reserved different roles in his theory of the understanding

for three different types of qualities. Examples of primary quali-
ties are the '*Bulk, Figure, Number, Situation,* and *Motion, or Rest* of'
(E II.viii.23) bodies (as well as solidity). Secondary qualities are the
'*Power that is in any Body,* by *Reason* of its insensible *primary
Qualities,* to operate after a peculiar manner on any of our Senses,
and thereby *produce in us* the *different Ideas* of several Colours,
Sounds, Smells, Tastes,' (ibid.). In addition, Locke briefly described
a third category of 'tertiary' qualities: 'the Power that is in any Body,
by Reason of the particular Constitution of its primary Qualities, to
make such a change in the Bulk, Figure, Texture, and Motion of
another Body, as to make it operate on our Senses, differently from
what it did before' (ibid.). Locke illustrated the third sort of quality
with: 'the Sun has a Power to make Wax White, and Fire to make
Lead fluid.'

Locke defines secondary and tertiary qualities as powers to do
something, to operate on the senses, or to make a change which
operates on the senses, whereas primary qualities are not defined as
powers to operate on the senses. This underscores a very important
difference between primary and secondary qualities when coupled
with the further important distinction between qualities and ideas of
qualities. If an object has a quality, say bulk, we then have an idea
of this quality caused by a quality which it represents. But secondary
and tertiary qualities are defined not as a distinct quality which then
may or may not cause an idea in the senses, but instead in relation to
the idea.

This asymmetry between primary qualities on the one hand and
secondary and tertiary qualities on the other raises the question of
whether the idea is always caused by the quality which the idea represents. According to Locke, primary qualities and the way that
they are arranged are the causes of the ideas of secondary and tertiary
qualities. Ideas of primary qualities represent real features or qualities of bodies communicated to us by the senses: they are natural
signs that resemble qualities in the external world, whereas secondary
and tertiary qualities are rather different. A secondary quality is a
set of primary qualities, ultimately reducible to relations among
primary qualities, which causes or disposes the senses to experience
a particular idea. For example, an experience of red is caused by the
arrangements of properties of light and the ways in which light inter-
acts with various media, including the eye. Note that on this account
there is no 'particular experience of red' anywhere but in the

perceiver, there are only different organized primary qualities out there in the external world. Yet, at the same time, the 'particular experience of red' can be explained causally in terms of '*Bulk, Figure, Number, Situation*, and *Motion, or Rest*'.

We can see then that Locke's distinction is an explanatory distinction which does service to an insight about differences among the content of ideas. It is amenable to the new science and the corpuscularian physics of Robert Boyle, but does not commit to one ontology or physical theory. At the same time, Locke allows that there is something mental and qualitatively irreducible about experiences of colour and pain. That there is an explanation of how I experience red does not mean that it explains the particular qualitative features of the experience of red. Even if there is an explanation in principle, it does not mean that I or any other finite creature can ever access it.

What is the basis for the distinction between primary and secondary (or tertiary qualities)? Boyle's and Descartes' distinctions are rooted in Galileo's division between (1) qualities which are mind dependent and qualities which are real or out there – 'I think if ears, tongues, and noses were taken away, shapes and numbers and motions would remain, but not odours or tastes or sounds. These, I believe, are nothing but names, apart from the living animal.'[22] Additionally, given that the distinction was advocated by these central early modern scientific theorists and experimentalists, it is not surprising that primary qualities have (2) an explanatory efficacy in the atomistic new sciences that secondary qualities do not. To quote one of my late teachers: 'A physics based on colours might be beautiful but if my doctor told me that the angioplasty machine he was about to use on me had been designed with a colour-based physics, I would jump from the operating table and run for my life.' This is connected to the sense we have that comparisons between primary qualities can be made with a much greater degree of precision than comparisons among secondary qualities, and in fact can be used to make the latter subject for more precise comparison (*E* IV.2.11).

Primary qualities tend to cause ideas of primary qualities (3), which are perceived by multiple senses. We can feel and see extended bodies, while ideas of secondary qualities tend to be ideas of a single sense. Primary qualities (4) persist under division and other sorts of transformation.[23] In his famous wax argument, Descartes held that we can modify a lump of wax so it no longer has a smell or a taste, or a colour, but we cannot modify it so that it will no longer have any extension.[24]

All of these justifications for the distinction between ideas of primary qualities and ideas of secondary quality identify primary qualities with permanence and ideas of secondary qualities with mind dependence and transience.[25] But why presume that ideas of primary qualities represent primary qualities in such a way that their permanence and mind independence are beyond doubt? And why presume that secondary qualities are reducible to arrangements of primary qualities when we can't access exactly how this works?

In a passage that Berkeley noted with interest, Malebranche pointed to the quandary:

Our eyes represent colours to us on the surface of bodies and light in the air and in the sun; our ears make us hear sounds as if spread out through the air and in the resounding bodies; and if we believe what the other senses report, heat will be in fire, sweetness will be in sugar, musk will have an odour, and all the sensible qualities will be in the bodies that seem to exude or diffuse them. Yet it is certain . . . that all these qualities do not exist outside the soul that perceives them – at least it is not evident that they are in the bodies that surround us. Why should we conclude then, merely on the testimony of the senses that deceive us on all sides, that there really are external bodies, and even that bodies are like those we see, i.e., like those that are the soul's immediate object, when we look at them with the eyes of the body.[26]

Malebranche notes that we perceive colours as spatially extended and 'on' bodies and sounds as 'spread out through the air'. If this is the case, why should we have faith either that states of bodies (or primary qualities) are accurately represented by their ideas, or indeed that bodies exist at all?

Berkeley considers each of the different senses – touch, taste, smell, sound, and sight. He begins with the idea of the secondary qualities 'heat and cold' (Descartes' examples of materially false and confused ideas), in order to draw out what he takes to be the incoherence at the core of the modern position. Berkeley's overarching strategy is clear from the outset. Instead of beginning with primary qualities as foundational and as representing the external world, and then moving to ideas of primary qualities, secondary qualities, and ideas of secondary qualities, Berkeley instead begins with ideas of secondary qualities such as colour, and then draws on their mind-dependent nature in order to attack their putative anchor out there in the mind-independent world of atoms or extension.

In *Essay* II.3 Locke distinguished between four kinds of ideas: (1) ideas of one sense; (2) ideas of more than one sense; (3) ideas of reflection; and (4) ideas 'suggested to the mind *by all the ways of Sensation and Refelection'* (*E* II.3.1). Each sense has ideas in the first category: 'The most considerable of those belonging to Touch, are Heat and Cold, and Solidity; all the rest, consisting almost wholly in the sensible Configuration, as smooth and rough; or else more, or less firm adhesion of the Parts, as hard and soft, tough and brittle are obvious enough' (ibid.). Locke then goes on to devote an entire section to ideas of solidity, the idea 'we receive more constantly from Sensation' than any other (*E* II.4.1). Solidity is crucial for Locke in that it is a basic (perhaps the basic) property of bodies, and although Locke does not explicitly refer to it as a primary quality it seems that he viewed it as an exemplary primary quality. For Locke solidity, as opposed to 'hardness', is not just a relational property of bodies ('I am made of feathers so that pillow feels mighty hard'), but instead appears to be an intrinsic non-relational property of all bodies. But what of heat and cold?

Locke offers heat and cold as exemplary secondary qualities and argues that their paradoxical features can best be explained with a corpuscularian theory:

> Ideas being thus distinguished and understood, we may be able to give an Account, how the same Water, at the same time, may produce the *Idea* of Cold by one Hand, and of Heat by the other: Whereas it is impossible, that the same Water, if those *Ideas* were really in it, should at the same time be both Hot and Cold. For if we imagine *Warmth*, as it is *in our Hands*, to be *nothing but a certain sort and degree of Motion in the minute Particles of our Nerves, or animal Spirits*, we may understand, how it is possible, that the same Water may at the same time produce the Sensation of Heat in one Hand, and Cold in the other. (*E* II.8.21)

The quote makes clear how much of the explanation rests on minute, unperceived, mind independent bodies, and how much the 'real existence' of secondary qualities depends on them on Locke's account. This is the position that Berkeley's Hylas will advocate in the *Dialogues*, once he has been disabused of a naive theory of sense perception where 'Heat therefore, if it be allowed a real being, must exist without the mind' (*D* 175, 30). Of course, Locke, Descartes, Malebranche, and others did not hold that our perception of heat, or our idea of heat, is in the fire.[27] Rather, Berkeley's arguments can be understood as an internal critique of the modern positions of Locke and Malebranche, which shows that the modern position suffers from the same defects as the older theories that they critique – whether Scholastic or modern, they seek to anchor the reality of ideas outside of the mind.

Philonous used two aspects of our perceptions of heat and cold to undermine Hylas' position: that heat and cold come in degrees (and in fact are extremes linked by degrees), and that perceptions of pain and pleasure go along with (and are often indistinguishable from) the perception of heat and cold. That pain and pleasure go along with all (or almost all) of our perceptions is Lockean (*E* II.7.2) and connected with natural law doctrines. Pains and pleasures motivate our action in that we desire goods and avoid evils. Reflection on pains and pleasures – some remote (the yawning, fiery pits of hell), some proximate (this tasty chocolate), some great (a good job after college), and some small (a night on the town) – sets out laws for our interactions with others and guides our conduct. Through pain and pleasure, rules have been woven into the world that are essential to our ultimate happiness and purpose.

If you accept that our painful perceptions are identical to extreme perceptions of sense qualities, then there's a serious problem for the Lockean. Although a rational person might think that hot and cold are in a fire, just as they might think that red is *on* the table, hardly anyone will claim that pain is in a fire, even if the fire occasions a great deal of pain. Pain seems to wholly depend on a perceiver. But if that is the case, then whatever sense quality pain is identical with – heat in this case – also depends on the perceiver.

But you might just say that our perception of 'OUCH!' is independent of our perception of 'hot', even though they often feel to us like 'HOT!' Locke held that the idea of a pain or a pleasure was distinct from the idea or ideas that accompanied it. This seems to be a dispute about the phenomenology, but how would one adjudicate it?[28] In response, Berkeley has Philonous set out a challenge to Hylas:

> Try in your thoughts, Hylas, if you can conceive a vehement sensation to be without pain, or pleasure . . . Or can you frame to yourself an idea of sensible pain or pleasure in general, abstracted from every particular idea of heat, cold, tastes, smells (*D* II: 177).

Hylas quickly admits that he cannot conceive of pain or pleasure in general.

In framing the challenge, Philonous uses the word 'abstracted'. In order to understand why Berkeley might think that one cannot frame pain or pleasure independent of a particular sense experience, we need to consider Berkeley's attack on abstract ideas.

A first stab at abstract ideas

When Berkeley first presented his immaterialism to the public in the *Principles*, he introduced his arguments with an attack on abstraction. He chose not to give his criticisms of abstraction such pride of place in the *Dialogues*: but not because he had rescinded his arguments in the three years that had elapsed. As we have just seen, Berkeley refers to abstraction at a crucial and early point in his argument in the *Dialogues*. Furthermore, he thought the arguments sufficiently important to include them in a similar form 20 years later in *Alciphron*. He also continued to hold that 'abstract ideas' were the source of much philosophical confusion in other later works, for example arguing in *De Motu* that many errors in natural philosophy among his contemporaries were due to the false belief that 'movement' could be abstracted from the perception of a particular moving thing. Perhaps Berkeley thought that, although correct and important, the somewhat technical discussion of abstraction had been an impediment to the reception of the *Principles*. It had stopped the physicians and bishops, whose negative reactions Sir John Percival had related in his letter to Berkeley, from pressing on beyond the 'Introduction', and they were left with the title, the table of contents, and vague, suspicious thoughts about what lay within. Still, since abstraction plays a role at key points in Berkeley's arguments in the ·*Dialogues* and elsewhere, we should consider his arguments against it. Be forewarned that the discussion that follows occasionally lapses into somewhat technical detail.

Berkeley's discussion of abstraction in the *Principles* is primarily framed as an attack on Locke, although he was highly critical of Malebranche's use of abstract ideas as well. Locke used 'abstraction' in the *Essay* primarily to mean separated from or removed from (IV.11.1, 618.).[29] He also defined 'abstraction' more narrowly as the capacity

> whereby Ideas taken from particular Beings, become general Representatives of all of the same kind; and their names general Names, applicable to whatever exists conformable to such abstract Ideas. Such precise, naked Appearances in the Mind, without considering, how, whence, or with what others they came there, the Understanding lays up (with Names commonly annexed to them) as the Standards to rank real Existences into sorts, as they agree with these Patterns, and to denominate them accordingly. (*E* II.11.9)

Ideas that designate or represent 'particular Beings' become 'general Representatives' through the power of abstraction. These general representatives are applied through general names that stand for the ideas and for whatever might fall under them. They are 'precise, naked' and allow us to rank and order 'real Existences'. The larger process of which abstraction is a part thus involves ideas and words, with the capacity or power of abstraction transforming ideas of particular beings into general representatives to which general names are then attached.

According to Berkeley, abstraction has 'had a chief part in rendering speculation intricate and perplexed, and to have occasioned innumerable errors and difficulties in almost all parts of knowledge' (*P* 'Introduction' 6). Locke had presumed that since under everyday circumstances words stand in for ideas and ideas represent 'real Existences' or things, if a 'general term' properly represents things there must be an intermediate abstract idea which it signifies and which in turn represents the thing (*P* 'Introduction,' 19; *A* 7.7). So just as if we use the name 'John Locke' properly, it must signify an idea we have of John Locke, which in turn represents the late, great philosopher, so also if we use 'triangle' generally and correctly it must signify the abstract general idea of 'triangle' (although it may not in turn refer to a thing).[30]

How did Berkeley think Locke understood the process of abstraction by which we acquire abstract ideas? We all perceive bundled, complex ideas through our senses, which include ideas of different qualities. When we perceive a snowball, for example, we take in simple ideas of qualities mixed together in a complex idea: cold, hard, white, and so forth. We use our capacity for abstraction to separate these pure, simple, abstract ideas out of the blend of qualities we experience in 'snowball'. Each quality – 'white', 'cold', 'hard' – is considered 'abstracted from those other qualities with which it is united' (*P* 'Introduction' 7). This is the first stage of the process leading to abstract ideas. Next, by leaving out or separating whatever distinguishing features make the idea of this white a particular shade of white, and the idea of this cold a particular shade of cold, we further abstract from particular images or ideas. The 'mind by leaving out of the particular colours perceived by sense, that which distinguishes them from one another, and retaining that only which is common to all, makes an idea of colour in abstract which is neither red, nor blue, nor white, nor any other determinate colour', but 'something common and alike in all' (*P* 'Introduction' 8).[31] We no longer have just an idea of a snowball, an extended entity flying towards us, but through a process of alchemy abstract ideas of 'this white', 'white' and then 'colour'.

Berkeley did not deny that we can distinguish particular features or qualities in a complex idea. I can distinguish: (1) 'a buggy' from 'a horse' in an idea of 'a horse and buggy'; or (2) 'a blue stripe' from 'a flag' in an idea of 'a flag with blue stripe'; or (3) 'blue' and 'stripe' from 'a blue stripe'. The cases are different, but Berkeley thinks that we have an unfortunate tendency to elide them. In the first two cases (the buggy and the flag), we hold that the objects distinguished *can* exist separately in some sense because they often *do* exist separately – there are buggies without horses and flags without blue stripes.

But now consider the example of the blue stripe. I can conceive of a stripe, and I can conceive of a splotch of blue. But can I conceive of a stripe which is not blue but also not another determinate colour (for then I would just be conceiving a 'red stripe' or a 'taupe stripe')? I might think I can because I can conceive a horse without a buggy and a flag without a blue stripe. Berkeley is criticizing this sort of move, where we go from ideas that we presume have objects which can be separated (because they often are) and infer that we can actually separate an idea into distinct parts of ideas (each of which is an idea) or qualities which in turn have distinct objects. In his discussion of abstraction in *Alciphron* Berkeley criticized the 'current Opinion that every substantive Name marks out and exhibits to the Mind one distinct Idea separate from all the others' (*A* VII.8). Due to this opinion we draw the false inference that all names denote contents of ideas, which are or can become ideas, which can then be separated. And we are led by a questionable inference to believe that we actually *can* conceive a stripe which is 'not-blue', when in fact we can do no such thing.

It appears to be logically possible that a stripe could be 'not-blue', i.e., lacking in all colour, and that we can abstract it in the mind even if it cannot exist separately in reality.[32] Yet Berkeley would say that you cannot mentally abstract the idea of 'stripe' that is not coloured.[33] The question is: Why? Berkeley's rejection of abstraction seems related to his rejection of a tacit premise that our ideas can be chopped or separated unproblematically into further sub-ideas. Berkeley thought that once we began chopping our ideas in this manner, they lose any content. Just as we wouldn't expect that if we separate 'stripe' further into 'stri' and 'pe' that we then have an idea of *stri* and an idea of *pe* latent in the idea of *stripe* so we wouldn't expect to imagine a stripe's length without its width. One reason that Berkeley may have thought that Locke's theory of abstraction allowed ideas that were in fact inseparable to be separated is Locke's assumption that, since we build up complex ideas from simple ideas, we should be able to abstract simple ideas from complex ideas. This may lead to a false confidence (in cases like the 'not-blue stripe') that we have separated a simple idea from a complex idea, when in fact we have distinguished between contents which are in fact inseparable.[34] But it is not obvious *why* they are inseparable.

We ought then to look further at how Locke thought that the process worked. In *Essay* IV Locke claimed about abstract ideas and the process leading to them that:

> When we reflect upon them, we shall find, that general *Ideas* are Fictions and Contrivances of the Mind, that carry difficulty with them, and do not easily offer themselves, as we are apt to imagine. For example, Does it not require some pain and skill to form the *general Idea* of a Triangle (which is yet none of the most abstract, comprehensive, and difficult) for it must be neither Oblique, nor Rectangle, neither Equilateral, Equicrural, nor Scalenon; but all

and none of these at once. In effect, it is something imperfect, that cannot exist; an Idea wherein some parts of several different and inconsistent Ideas are put together. 'Tis true, the Mind in this imperfect state, has need of such *Ideas*, and makes all the haste to them it can, for the conveniency of Communication, and Enlargement of Knowledge; to both which, it is naturally very much enclined. But yet one has reason to suspect such Ideas are marks of our Imperfection; at least this is enough to shew, that the most abstract and general Ideas, are not those that the Mind is *first* and most easily acquainted with, nor such as its Knowledge is conversant about. (*E* IV.7.9)

Locke viewed these abstract general ideas as achievements: difficult achievements, which separate human beings from animals and adults from children. At the same time, he avoided an account of abstract ideas that smacked of excessive Platonism. Locke stressed that abstract, general ideas were non-existent fictions – difficult both to form and to characterize – but important and distinctive to rational beings nonetheless.

Berkeley began his criticisms of Locke in the *Principles* by denying Locke's presumption that we can conceive of abstract ideas at all. Berkeley responded that, try as we might, we cannot form the idea of a general triangle that is neither an isosceles nor a scalene nor some other particular triangle. Instead, when we do try to form an abstract, general triangle we always end up perceiving the idea of this or that particular triangle. This is the same strategy that Berkeley used in the passage we have just considered from the *Dialogues* concerning the inseparability of pain from particular sense perceptions (and will use in a number of other ways later on). In this case we are separating two qualities, pain and heat, as opposed to a triangle and the determinate way in which it is a triangle (or blue from the blue stripe in my example), but the similar forms of the challenges suggests that the problems with conceiving them are related.

On the surface at least, Berkeley does not provide much of an argument. I may live among people incapable of forming abstract ideas, and I may be incapable of forming them, but that doesn't mean that *no one* is capable of conceiving them, much the less that they are inconceivable (which is a different issue from whether anyone does happen to conceive them). To extend Locke's point about achievement, it might just be a reflection of the fact that I and all those I know are not particularly high achievers. This doesn't show that abstract ideas can't be conceived. Consequently, if you have Berkeley-like intuitions and you feel that his point about the inconceivability of abstract ideas is correct – i.e., you are unable to conceive an abstract idea in Locke's sense and you infer that others are incapable of this as well *because* they are inconceivable – you would still need to explain *why* they are inconceivable if you were to be able to rule them out.

One reason why they might be inconceivable is that it might be impossible to think an abstract idea if it was a complex idea made up of ideas that contradicted one another – like 'square circle'. We can't think 'square circle' because the geometrical formula or description of square commits us to 'not circle' and vice versa. 'Square circle' wears its contradictory character on its sleeve, so to speak, since it combines two simple geometrical objects, the definition of each which excludes the other (as opposed to 'closed circle' or 'right-angled square'). But perhaps similar contradictions are smuggled into our more complicated abstract ideas: contradictions which arise from the process of abstraction itself. Berkeley would have been developing a suggestion from Locke (since Locke seems to have allowed that abstract ideas might be conflicted or contradictory) by admitting that abstract ideas put together 'parts of several different and inconsistent Ideas' and suggesting that this may be why they are fictions. Admittedly, 'inconsistent' does not mean the same as 'contradictory to conceive': it is at most impossible to realize outside of the mind since they are inconsistent when put together.

Berkeley's arguments imply that if 'colour' is an example of an abstract idea, and if it is supposed to be simple, pure and abstracted from any particular sense perception, then the abstract idea 'colour' is neither red, nor blue, nor any other colour, yet it represents all at once; 'food' is neither a madeleine, nor a carrot stick, nor any other food, yet it represents all food (*P* 'Introduction' 13). Yet, since it is abstracted from particular ideas, and derives its contents from these ideas, it must share something with them. But any way we look at the particular ideas from which we abstract our abstract general ideas, we just find the particular qualitative properties of these ideas (or for Berkeley the particular qualitative properties which *are* these ideas). So if we look at our idea of 'this red' and we inspect its content, we just find, well, homogenous 'this red'. Therefore the general idea insofar as it is derived from 'this red' and stands in for 'this red' must both be and yet not be 'this red', since it is also 'this blue', 'this chartreuse' and so forth. Then it must both be 'this red' and 'not this red'. Consequently it is impossible to conceive. Unfortunately, there are a number of problems here. First, Berkeley doesn't really offer an argument like this: he just states that we can't find an idea like this anywhere in our thoughts. And second, it is not clear that this really is a contradiction or that it renders the idea inconceivable. As Mackie points out: 'I can consider a man as having stature without there being any particular stature I consider him as having, and likewise colour.'[35] What contradiction there is seems to rest on a strong thesis about ideas, which claims that they are images either acquired through the senses directly or derived from other images. It certainly could be the case that we can only perceive particular images, and some (like Ayers) hold that this is Locke's position as well: but then all Berkeley's 'argument' really says is that we can't form abstract ideas from particular images because that's not how the images specific to each of our senses are. The obvious retort is: Why presume that all that we perceive are particular images?

There might be less contingent but related reasons to reject abstract ideas.[36] Martha Bolton has argued that the rejection of abstract ideas follows from a different commitment of Berkeley's theory of ideas, and his arguments that ideas are not distinct from objects which they represent. If 'an abstract idea is its own object and thus has all the properties its object does; . . . it must also lack some of those properties, because it is supposed to omit some properties of its object(s)' and it is consequently impossible.[37] So the idea of the triangle must both have all the properties of a scalene triangle (which is its object) and lack some of these properties. Since Berkeley's primary objection to abstract ideas was that we cannot 'conceive separately, those qualities which it is impossible should exist so separated' (P 'Introduction' 10), what can't be separated on Bolton's view is the abstract idea and its particular representative content. The problem with this version of abstraction is that it rests on one of the main achievements of Berkeley's *Principles*: the denial that ideas have objects distinct from them which they represent, and this at best makes Berkeley's claim that the errors of the modern philosophers arise from their conceptions of abstract ideas hyperbole.

Winkler argues, conversely but similarly, that as long as the abstractionist 'accepts the content assumption' – i.e., 'the assumption that the content of thought is determined by its object' – then 'any difference between *conceiving of triangularity apart from particular triangles* and *conceiving of the separate existence of triangularity* can only depend on differences in the corresponding objects of thought.' So my thoughts about rocks depend on rocks for their distinctive properties if they have some rocks in the external world as their object (*a la* Locke), or my thoughts about '2 + 2 = 4' depend on some further objective idea of '2 + 2 = 4' for whatever properties they have (*a la* Malebranche), and so forth.

'But' according to Winkler, 'it is not obvious what difference in the objects could account for the difference in content.' In other words, it is not clear how a difference in a scalene triangle and an isosceles triangle could account for whatever is the distinctive content of the abstract idea of 'triangle'. It would seem that the differences between scalene and isosceles triangles would just account for scalene properties and isosceles properties. Winkler concludes: 'Berkeley's argument therefore presents an explanatory challenge to anyone who accepts the content assumption whether or not he or she believes that ideas are images.'[38] According to Winkler, Berkeley further holds that if abstract ideas are inconceivable, then they are impossible if one holds that the content of thought is determined by its object – as both Locke and Malebranche did.

In making sense of Locke's claim that abstract ideas are imperfect and cannot exist, we can draw on Winkler's diagnosis of what Berkeley saw as their root imperfection: that they cannot have the distinctive sorts of contents that Locke and others attribute to them, but rather are inconceivable and non-existent, not just inconsistent.[39] This solution has the advantage over Bolton's of not depending on a particular process (Lockean abstraction) or a particular doctrine (Berkeley's own theory of ideas). It also provides a general criticism of abstraction, which can then be used against one of Berkeley's main targets, Newton, who provided no general doctrine of abstraction yet used abstraction at a key moment in the *Principia* (as we will soon discuss). It has the disadvantage, as with Bolton's argument, that it rests abstraction on a thesis about representation that only enters somewhat tangentially into Berkeley's main discussion.

Let's return now to our particular passage from the *Dialogues*, on the separability of pain or pleasure from other particular ideas of the senses:

> Try in your thoughts, Hylas, if you can conceive a vehement sensation to be without pain, or pleasure . . . Or can you frame to

yourself an idea of sensible pain or pleasure in general, abstracted from every particular idea of heat, cold, tastes and smell. (*D* 176–7)

Whether pain and pleasure and particular sense experiences are inseparable is questionable: there are reports of people who claim to experience vehement sensations but not to feel any pain or pleasure. But Berkeley certainly thought that they were inseparable. He suggests that we cannot frame an abstract idea of pain and pleasure because we cannot conceive of a pain independent of a vehement sensation, and of a vehement sensation independent of a pain or pleasure. This implies that Berkeley sees not just a relation but some kind of essential connection between the two sensations. Hume later held that what was inseparable was identical, and the bi-conditional form of the challenge intimates that Berkeley may have held something like this as well.[40] Returning to Winkler's account, we can then say that we cannot abstract the qualities of vehement heat or other vehement sensations from pain and hold an abstract idea of pain because there seems to be no way to distinguish pain from a particular vehement perception, and no differences among the particular vehement perceptions explain what is in 'pain' and yet not in any of the perceptions.

Berkeley concluded the discussion of abstract ideas in the *Principles*:

We have, I think, shewn the impossibility of *abstract ideas*. We have considered what has been said for them by their ablest patrons; and endeavoured to shew they are of no use for those ends, to which they are thought necessary. And lastly we have traced them to the source from whence they flow, which appears to be language. (*P* 'Introduction' 21)

Even if abstract ideas are impossible, it is clear that we use 'pain', 'pleasure', and other general terms all the time. In the case of pain and pleasure, thinking in general about pains and pleasures was central for Berkeley to what mattered most – what kind of life we should choose, what will truly make us happy, etc. So it will not do just to say pain or pleasure do not exist because they are abstract ideas, and be done with it. It is also apparent that we can know truths about triangles or pains and pleasures that hold true of all particular triangles or of all pains and pleasures. So it seems not just out of touch with our ordinary practices to banish general talk, but a bit mad. Locke was rightly reluctant to do this. Berkeley did not wish to rid language of all generalities: indeed, it was integral to his argument.

Berkeley thought that the licit functions of abstract ideas could be better explained by determinate ideas of sense or images and language, without recourse to occult entities or to a distinct faculty of or capacity for abstraction. I think this is key for understanding his challenge. Recall that Locke began his *Essay* with a discussion of innate ideas. And, further recall that Berkeley thought that the way in which Locke began the *Essay* had an unfortunate founding effect on the subsequent argument. Berkeley clearly began the *Principles* with an attack on abstract ideas in order to set it on the right course, in opposition to the beginning of Locke's *Essay*. From Berkeley's brief remark in the *Notebooks,* it cannot be concluded precisely where he thought the problem lay.[41] A plausible interpretation would be that he thought that the rejection of innate ideas (ideas that are not derived from experience) led Locke to infer that ideas represent things or processes in an external world beyond immediate perception, and consequently the most important ideas were mind independent.[42] This problem was ramified with Book II, and aggravated by discussion of abstract ideas where, again, ideas somehow had contents above or beyond particular mind-dependent perceptions. Had Locke begun with Book III, he would have recognized that the curtain of words is very thick and that we partition the world more along the lines of our own interests, and this is reflected in our language. With his more deflationary side and nominalist leanings prominent at the outset, Locke might not have thought that we have access to purified abstract ideas. Berkeley thought that by providing reasons why abstract ideas ought to be rejected he could set the *Principles* on the good footing that Locke's *Essay* lacked because of its ill-advised order.

And there's a further structural parallel. Locke introduced his criticisms of innate ideas by noting: 'it would be sufficient to convince unprejudiced Readers of the falseness of this Supposition, if I could only shew . . . how Men, barely by the Use of their natural Faculties, may attain to all the Knowledge they have, without the help of any innate Impressions; and may arrive at Certainty without any such Original Notions or Principles' (*E* I.2.1). Locke tried to show that innate ideas were inconsistent and that even if they could exist they might be better explained differently, and that this was sufficient to rule them out. Berkeley, in the same spirit, wished to show that abstract ideas were impossible, for any of a number of reasons, but more importantly that their function could be explained without recourse to a questionable mental process or faculty-generating occult entities. This was crucial for his overall argument. Even if Berkeley's challenge seems dubious, if Berkeley can provide an alternative explanation that has fewer presuppositions and leads to fewer paradoxes – much like the criterion that Philonous set out at the beginning of the *Dialogues* – then his account is to be preferred.

Berkeley argued that when I prove a general proposition about a triangle, although the triangle I have in mind is particular – an isosceles, or a scalene, or some other particular sort of triangle – I can know that the proof will hold generally of all triangles, because 'neither the right angle, nor the equality, nor the determinate length of the sides, are at all concerned in the demonstration' since 'a man may consider a figure merely as triangular, without attending to the particular qualities of the angles, or relations of the sides.' In this passage Berkeley is describing a process which Mackie called 'selective attention', where we attend to particular features of an image as we would to different parts of a painting. We're not separating, just focusing our attention and using different words to describe the different ways that we attend to our ideas. This allows Berkeley to mirror the process of abstraction without recourse to separating out different ideas. Instead, I just call a particular aspect of my vehement sensation of heat 'pain,' i.e., that it makes me yell and plunge my hand in cold water.

Given the embrace of selective attention as opposed to abstraction, Berkeley did not want to use the term 'abstract idea', so instead he used the term 'general idea'. By general ideas he understood ideas used to organize more than one particular image to some functional end. A Berkeleyan general idea is not arrived at through the mental process of abstraction, but is made to function generally by standing in for and signifying other ideas: 'a black line, for instance, an inch long, though in itself particular, may yet become universal, being used as a sign to stand for any line whatsoever' (A VII.7; P 'Introduction' 12). Or a black line might stand for a group of particular experiences that have nothing to do with lines. The relation does not depend on the process of abstraction, nor on a mental entity which represents a pure, general content shared by particular, determinate ideas. Consequently, there is an alternative explanation with less premises and less paradoxical consequences, and it should be preferred.

There is something counterintuitive about this, though. It does seem as if shades of red are red by virtue of the fact that they are all, well, red! Even the analogy he offers, the black line, signifies due to resemblance – a one inch line stands for any line. But if there is resemblance then it seems Berkeley does presuppose an abstract idea of red.

One solution, associated with Hume, would be that resemblances are always between particular experiences, and so between comparisons of particular shades of red:

> 'Tis evident, that even different simple ideas may have a similarity or resemblance to each other; nor is it necessary, that the point or circumstances of resemblance shou'd be distinct or separable from that in which they differ. Blue and green are different simple ideas, but are more resembling than blue and scarlet; tho' their perfect simplicity excludes all possibility of separation or distinction. (*T* 1.1.7.6).

There is nothing in Berkeley's argument to rule out pursuing the Humean solution: comparing objects of one sense pairwise, and making judgments about their resemblance. In fact, that we can talk about degrees of vehemence of sensations at all presumes such comparisons. This is quite different from saying that there is an abstract idea separable from all of these particular comparisons.

If this is consistent, then Berkeley did not hold that all relations we discover are arbitrary for us in the sense of willy-nilly or unstable (although even these could have been otherwise). Berkeley thought that Locke had confused consistent, stable but arbitrary signification with a natural sign: that the ideas which he thought to naturally signify objects preserve their natural signification when abstracted in any of a variety of ways because of the compositional character of ideas (as presented above in the example of the snowball). This in turn arose from the presumption that words always stand 'as outward Marks of our internal *Ideas*' (E II.11.9), i.e., that if I have the word 'red' and can use it meaningfully there must be an abstract idea of 'red' removed from a composite and which refers to something – in this case to the many red objects. Berkeley held instead that 'though indeed we are apt to think every noun substantive stands for a distinct ideas, that may be separated from all the others: which hath occasioned infinite mistakes' (*P* 116). He did not think that this was solely a problem for Locke's metaphysics and epistemology, but that it also had consequences for his moral theory and his philosophical theology. The discussion of abstraction in *Alciphron* is, surprisingly for us but not for Berkeley's contemporaries, initiated and then followed by a discussion of Christian faith.

In contradistinction, Berkeley thought that words:

> should not, every time they are used, excite the ideas they signify in our minds; it being sufficient that we have it in our power to substitute things or ideas for their signs when there is occasion. It seems also to follow, that there may be another use of words besides that of marking and suggesting distinct ideas, to wit, the influencing our conduct and actions; which may be done either by forming rules for us to act by, or by raising certain passions, dispositions, and emotions in our minds. A discourse, therefore, that directs how to act or excites to the doing or forebearance of an action may, it seems, be useful and significant, although the words whereof it is composed should not bring each a distinct idea into our minds. (*A* VII.8)[43]

This quote provides the outline of an account of language that we will discuss in greater detail later on. It is apparent that Berkeley thought that the Lockean account of language obscured a different function of language, 'the influencing our conduct and actions; which may be done either by forming rules for us to act by, or by raising certain passions, dispositions, and emotions in our minds', and that this misled us into thinking that if words are separable then so are ideas and things, since it is 'a current Opinion that every substantive Name marks out and exhibits to the Mind one distinct Idea separate from all the others' (*A* VII.8).

More about the senses and sensory qualities (176–188)
As we've seen, Berkeley uses Philonous' challenge to Hylas to frame an abstract idea of pain and pleasure separated from particular

sense perceptions, and to then argue that heat and cold fall on the mind–dependent side. This argument is sometimes described as an *assimilation argument*,[44] in that heat and cold are assimilated to pain and pleasure (although it depends on a prior premise about abstraction). Berkeley might have had us consider the vision of a shocking colour of mauve that causes us pain: but 'mauve' is less amenable to his argument then 'heat' and 'cold' because less intuitively connected to pain and pleasure. One intriguing consequence of the inseparability or identity of pain and pleasure from particular sensations would be that pains and pleasures will differ as the senses differ – i.e., each of the senses will have their pains and pleasure that can then be organized under general ideas, as opposed to pain and pleasure having one distinct content that is independent of particular sense contents.

Hylas is quickly disabused of the naive belief (or just pre-modern belief, in that it was held by Aristotle and others) that extreme heat can exist without the mind, i.e., that extreme heat is in objects. But, even if vehement heat is clearly mind dependent because it is inseparable from pain, it is far less evident that lesser degrees of heat are in the mind. Philonous uses examples from Locke and Malebranche[45] to attack this position. In introducing heat and cold, Locke stated that 'water may at the same time produce the Sensation of Heat in one Hand, and Cold in the other'. Echoing Locke, Philonous then argued that since it would be absurd to think that the same thing was both hot and cold, heat and cold cannot be in the water (or in any object). This argument is sometimes described as an *argument from illusion* in that the experiences of pain or pleasure are shown to be illusory since the same water result in different (even opposed) perceptions.[46] The argument from illusion was taken by Berkeley-inspired philosophers such as Ayer to show that, since some perceptions are illusory, we can infer that we do not perceive physical states, but rather that we perceive something else. Although Berkeley would be happy with this result, he will need further argument to get there! As it stands the present argument is unconvincing for a less sophisticated reason: the physical states or structure of each hand may differ, explaining the different perceptions without entailing any contradiction.[47]

But regardless of these possible objections, Hylas is convinced, and enters the modern era with the confidence 'that there still remain qualities enough to secure the reality of external things'. And indeed, the analysis of the physiognomy of heat, distinguishing between mechanistic physical causes and perception, was a triumph of early modern natural philosophy and medicine. Philonous gives him a warning of what is to come with the comment: 'But what will you say, Hylas, if it shall appear that the case is the same with regard to all the other sensible qualities, and that they can no more be supposed to exist without the mind, than heat and cold'; and he soon moves in succession through discussions of taste, smell, sound, and colour, briskly dispensing with three senses (taste, smell, sound) and two qualities (colour, heat/cold) in just a few pages. Sight and touch have a special place in Locke's account (and those of Descartes and others), in that Locke identified primary qualities with qualities like extension, which he held that we can both see and touch.

Some of the arguments that Philonous employs are similar to those he used against heat and cold. Philonous shows Hylas that sweetness and bitterness can be assimilated to pleasure and pain, just as heat and cold can. Just as the same object can feel hot to one hand and cold to the other, so also two people may disagree on whether the same food is sweet or bitter. He also draws on other Pyrrhonian modes like the 'argument from differences among animal' ('can you imagine, that filth and ordure affect those brute animals that feed on them out of choice, with the same smells which we perceive in them?' (*D* 181)). These arguments were stock and trade for the modern philosopher. Furthermore Locke, Malebranche, and Descartes all agreed that tastes, smells, sounds and colours are mind dependent, and all of these philosophers used Pyrrhonian techniques to undermine the mind independence of these qualities.

Sound and colour, however, seem closer to the real physical world of external things. When we look at a dappled pony it *looks* like the dapple is on the pony. When we hear the pony neigh from far away, the neighing *sounds* far away. Furthermore, just as was the case with heat, we have ready physical explanations. In claiming that sound can be identified with or reduced to motion, Hylas invokes Otto van Guericke's famous vacuum experiment (which showed that a bell in a vacuum made no sound) as evidence that 'air therefore must be thought the subject of sound' (*D* 181).[48] In addition, we can give a clear causal account of how sound arises in us: 'striking on the drum of the ear', the moving air 'causeth a vibration, which by the auditory nerves being communicated to the brain, the soul is thereupon affected with the sensation called *sound*' (*D* 181).

The same holds of colour. The great Newton himself gave a 'physical' explanation of colours, showing with the aid of a prism that the whole of the colour spectrum was in light. When discussing colour, Hylas first advocates what much of Berkeley's audience would consider to be a naive or pre-modern account of colours (colours are on objects); and then, with Philonous' criticism and aid, presents a Newton and Locke-inspired account.[49] Notably it is Philonous who introduces Newton's prism into the discussion. Berkeley is not attempting to undermine Newton's experimental results but rather to dispute the philosophical inferences that Newton and others drew from them.

Sounds and colours each have further properties that other senses and qualities do not. Sounds allow us to localize objects in space – 'that bull elephant charging at me still sounds like it's a good half mile away' – in relation to our ears. Even if we hear through another source, for example a microphone, we locate objects in space around the microphone. We seem not to do this with taste and smell. Philonous and Hylas do not discuss this aspect of sound. In fact, they dispense with sound quite quickly by employing another one of Berkeley's favourite arguments. Hylas argues that sound should be primarily identified with the mind-independent physical process leading up to us hearing the sound; and secondarily, with the mind-dependent perception of sound that we hear. But, as Philonous notes, we never hear the former. We do not hear air or waves or motions or vibrations – we see or feel them. If this is true then Hylas is in fact arguing that we cannot hear the most real sounds, we can only see or touch them. This qualifies as a sceptical paradox!

There is another kind of argument latent in these passages, which Berkeley will use shortly to secure some of his most famous doctrines: 'esse is percipi', and immaterialism. A thing 'A' cannot be related to another thing 'B', and by extension 'A' cannot cause 'B', if 'A' and 'B' are wholly dissimilar: like causes like, and unlike cannot cause unlike. Malebranche and Locke both held that causes presupposed similarity and that things which were wholly dissimilar could not be related as cause to effect, as did almost all other early modern philosophers (and ancient philosophers as well). If we add two additional premises: first, that there is no similarity between the senses of sound, and sight and touch,[50] and second, that motion is only known by sight and touch, then motion cannot cause sounds.

Berkeley wishes to move from the generic rule 'like causes like' to a thesis stipulating which way things must be alike for them to be related or to function as causes.[51] But, in spite of this, the argument in the *Dialogues* would fail if we could hear motions (although motions would then be sounds). To return to the example of the bull elephant, it seems that I *do* hear a bull elephant charging; that's why I run for my life! Berkeley will explain examples like this through association:

> For instance, when I hear a Coach drive along the Streets, immediately I perceive only the Sound; but from the Experience I have had that such a Sound is connected with a Coach, I am said to hear the Coach. It is nevertheless evident, that in truth and strictness, nothing can be heard but Sound: And the Coach is not then properly perceived by Sense, but suggested from Experience. (*D* II: 204, see also *NTV* 46)

Reasonable enough: but imagine that there is a person born without sight, who for whatever reason is born without a sense of touch either. Would they be able to judge distances on the basis of sound? It seems that they at least would be able to judge a threshold or a limit, for example they might be able to judge that 'however loud the report of the cannon, if it is far enough away, it will be out of earshot.'[52] If the sound is painful when not out of earshot, and I am able to turn my head away from the sound and diminish the pain, why couldn't I view this as a rudimentary conception of space?

We might criticize this thought experiment as drawing on the fact that the head can move in different directions, that this is somehow 'touch-like'. But the fact that we have ears on each side of our head, hear in stereo, and can move our heads is not simply reducible to sight or touch.[53] Berkeley tends to associate pain with touch, but it seems clear from the abstraction argument that pain can also arise from sounds, in that they too can be vehement sensations. Berkeley would probably respond that there is an added step in saying sound defines or is in a space moving from louder and quieter to closer and further. Imagine that instead of the sound being nearer and closer it is just louder and softer – you are wearing a pair of headphones for example. You need to correlate it to visual and tactile space.

Berkeley probably did not own a pair of headphones, so he would need to provide a different explanation, since he just seems to have taken it for granted that we do not hear distance in any sense (*NTV* 47). But at least he has begun to answer one of the questions I mentioned at the beginning of this book. If a tree falls in the forest, and there is no one there to hear it, it seems it would not have a sound. Whether there is a tree at all if no one perceives anything about it will have to be established later!

Colours pose a different problem. We see colour as interconnected with all sorts of other more (apparently) permanent information. Recall the quote from Malebranche: 'our eyes represent colours to us on the surface of bodies and light in the air and in the sun.' This is indeed too weak. We see the surfaces of bodies *as* coloured. This could make for a quick path to immaterialism, and Berkeley has Philonous try to draw this consequence for Hylas:

Philonous: Pray, is your corporeal Substance either a sensible Quality, or made up of sensible Qualities?
Hylas: What a Question that is! who ever thought it was?
Philonous: My Reason for asking was, because in saying, each visible Object hath that Colour which we see in it, you make visible Objects to be corporeal Substances; which implies either that corporeal Substances are sensible Qualities, or else that there is something beside sensible Qualities perceived by Sight: But as this Point was formerly agreed between us, and is still maintained by you, it is a clear Consequence, that your corporeal Substance is nothing distinct from sensible Qualities. (*D* II: 183)

In other words, if Hylas agrees that we perceive colours as belonging to objects, as parts, properties or predicates of objects (as opposed to as peculiarities of our visual systems), then either: (1) the colour is *not* the object (i.e., it is an accidental property of the object or corporeal substance, and something besides the sensible perception of colour must then *be* the object or corporeal substance); or (2) we must perceive something non-sensible which is the object or corporeal substance in order to perceive it as an object or as a corporeal substance. But (2) cannot be the case, since we only perceive sensible qualities with and through our senses. If you respond that the object or corporeal substance could be due to another sensible quality than colour (such as extension), the argument still goes through for the same reasons. Therefore a corporeal substance is only its sensible qualities.[54]

Philonous does not press the point, since Locke, Malebranche, Descartes, *et alii* did not hold that colours belong to objects in the sense Hylas briefly advocated. Berkeley's own view was in fact much closer to the position that Hylas surrenders for the modern view, and he remarked in the *Notebooks* that 'Men are in the right in judging their simple ideas to be in the things themselves, certainly Heat & colour is as much without the mind as figure, motion, time etc.' (*PC* 222). A basic problem for Berkeley is how to explain the unity that we experience objects and qualities to have without recourse to an unperceived or unperceivable cause of this unity.

This point was particularly important for Berkeley for a further reason, connected with the inseparability of pain and pleasure from particular sense perceptions. When Hylas adopted the position that colours are caused by and derivative of corpuscular motion, he tacitly assumed that the sounds we hear and the colours we see are *less real* than the motions that cause them (which are the 'real' sounds and colours), since all of the philosophers whose positions Hylas' position mirrors held that whatever is in the effect must be present at least as much, or in this case to a greater degree, in the cause.[55] Sensible perceptions are therefore derivative of, similar to but *less than* or impoverished in comparison with the mechanisms that produce them. To quote Robert Frost's 'Ovenbird', what then to make of this diminished thing?

Berkeley probably saw this line of argument as a particularly sorry example of how philosophers have reduced God's rich language by which he speaks to his subjects to just so much mechanism. Berkeley signals the importance of the point by having Hylas manage to irritate the normally imperturbable Philonous on this issue:

> Philonous: What! are then the beautiful red and purple we see on yonder clouds, really in them? Or do you imagine they have in themselves any other Form, than that of a dark mist or vapour?
> Hylas: I must own, Philonous, those colours are not really in the clouds as they seem to be at this distance. They are only apparent colours.
> Philonous: *Apparent* call you them? how shall we distinguish these apparent colours from real? (*D* II: 184)

Recall that Philonous began the 'First Dialogue' by remarking on 'the purple sky' to Hylas, and praising the beautiful morning. Cloistered Hylas is unable to 'see' beautiful red and purple because he is always looking for corpuscles and mechanisms beneath, and he seeks to assimilate beautiful appearances to these washed-out and fictive explanations. He has become incapable of attending to what the sensations are communicating to him in two ways. First, Berkeley's challenge to abstract an idea of pain from particular sense perceptions had the result (if the challenge argument is successful) that different pains and pleasures have different sense-specific content, insofar as they just are 'vehement' perceptions of this or that sense. By reducing all qualities to the content of a very few, and the ways in which they can be related, experience is peopled by diminished things.[56]

Second, much like Shaftesbury, Berkeley thought that this has moral consequences as well. A Lockean admits that 'pain' and 'pleasure' are the most important qualities for our life; but pain and pleasure now subordinate to primary qualities, so we can't 'see' the pleasure in purple clouds. Pains and pleasures also tend to be homogenized. Berkeley associated this sort of thinking with what early modern authors called 'Epicureanism': the belief that all action, and by extension all morality, are prompted by the satisfaction of homogeneous and hedonistic desires. Locke and Samuel Pufendorf (the famous natural lawyer whom Locke followed in these matters) presented theistic versions of Epicureanism. Mandeville presented a 'vulgar', atheistic version of it.

Consequently, there is a lot at stake for Berkeley, and he has Philonous do full service to his opponents' positions by submitting colour to the full sceptical arsenal: different animals perceive colours differently, colours appear different under a microscope (think of looking at a hair or a brightly coloured bird feather), an object's colour can change with a change of perspective, etc.

These arguments have been particularly strongly criticized. If colours are mind dependent then there is a serious problem in making sense of Berkeley's various claims that he is showing objects do have colours against the moderns. This will come to a head in our discussion of the 'Third Dialogue'. One way out is to show that Berkeley's arguments are less for mind dependence then against mind independence. This has an advantage if it is felt that Berkeley seems too quick to jump from the fact that I perceive something and that the perception is variable to its mind dependence. On this reading Berkeley's arguments for mind dependence of sense perceptions are in the voice of the modern philosopher and dialectical: his own position is beyond the false dichotomy that arises from a contrast between mind dependent and mind independent. Philonous is using sceptical techniques to undermine what Hylas offers him and to show that ideas of secondary qualities are not wholly mind independent. This definitely seems to have something right about it, although we will have to see whether it gets us out of the problems of the 'Third Dialogue'.[57]

A number of objections have been offered to Berkeley's arguments when they are construed as establishing the mind dependence of colours. First, I can and do easily distinguish between the primary colour an object has and variations. I can say a stripe is blue even if it is in fact a whole variety of colours as the flag flutters in the wind. Doesn't this then allow us to say that there is a real colour in the object, even if there is some mind-dependent variation?

Second, can't I say that the colour of an object is the colour under stipulated ideal conditions? To paraphrase a famous example from Wilfrid Sellars, if I go into a tie store pick up a tie which seems to me to be green and tell the cashier 'I wish to buy this green tie,' and if the cashier wishes to correctly disabuse me of my belief that the tie is green, he can tell me to look at the tie in the sunlight or under light conditions better than the dim store lighting. Upon returning from the outside I will say 'This tie seems green but it is blue,' and thus distinguish between how my perceptions *seem* and what they are really of by reference to a shared standard.[58] Berkeley could easily maintain that distinctions between a real colour and how the colour seems, or reference to an ideal standard, are susceptible to the same sorts of objections – that they are arbitrary stipulations and vary with our explanatory interests.

Under pressure of the arsenal of arguments, Hylas quickly acquiesces. He presents a new, fully modern thesis:

> I frankly own, Philonous, that it is in vain to stand out any longer. Colours, sounds, tastes, in a word, all those termed *secondary qualities*, have certainly, no existence without the mind. But by this acknowledgment I must not be supposed to derogate any thing from the reality of matter or external objects, seeing it is no more than several philosophers maintain, who nevertheless are

the farthest imaginable from denying matter. For the clearer Understanding of this, you must know sensible qualities are by Philosophers divided into *primary* and *secondary*. The former are extension, figure, solidity, gravity, motion, and rest. And these they hold exist really in bodies. The latter are those above enumerated; or briefly, all sensible qualities beside the primary, which they assert are only so many sensations or ideas existing no where but in the mind. But all this, I doubt not, you are already apprised of. For my part, I have been a long time sensible there was such an opinion current among philosophers, but was never thoroughly convinced of its truth till now. (*D* 187–8)

Primary qualities and abstraction revisited (188–94)

Many of Berkeley's criticisms of secondary qualities would have been happily embraced by Locke, Malebranche, Hobbes, Galileo, Descartes, and others. In fact, as we've seen, some of Berkeley's arguments were taken directly from these pillars of early modern philosophy. Berkeley's distinctive insight was that what held of secondary qualities held by extension of primary qualities, and that the very arguments that the modern advocates of the new science had employed against pre-modern philosophers who believed in the mind independence of secondary qualities could also be used against the existence of matter. This insight seems particularly appropriate for presentation in dialogue form, with its dialectical twists and turns. Hylas has been convinced of the modern position, but the very arguments that convinced him will now be used to undermine some of the position's central tenets. This is not to say that Berkeley wished to return philosophy to a golden age before Locke and Malebranche: obviously not. Rather Berkeley wished to show how the belief in the existence of mind-independent entities, above all in matter, had been reinforced by sloppy language (the curtain of words) and corrupting philosophical theories about the relation between mind and a mind-independent world. Although the errors persisted, the remedy was near.

Philonous initiates this section of the argument of the 'First Dialogue' by asking whether 'extension and figures are inherent in external unthinking substances'. *Unthinking* substances would also be *unperceiving* substances, so the question could be rephrased: 'Are extension and figure mind-independent qualities or properties?' As we have seen, from Galileo onwards properties had been tacitly divided into those that can exist without minds (like shape and extension) and those that can only exist when perceived (like odours and tastes). Over the course of the argument Berkeley has moved from the qualities which seem most mind dependent (pain, heat and cold, smells and tastes) to those which seem slightly more mind independent (colour, sound), and now to those which seem wholly mind independent (extension and figure).

Berkeley's predecessors and contemporaries did not agree on what exactly the relation was between matter and extension, and there were numerous variations on the thesis that extension and figure were inherent in unthinking substances. Some philosophers thought that bodies were made up of extended atoms and that extension was one of a *few* real qualities of bodies (Hobbes, Locke, Boyle), while others thought that bodies were extended plenums and extension was trivially inherent in bodies since their essence *was* extension (Descartes, Spinoza).

As we have seen, the modern position is not that all qualities are mind independent, but rather that mind-independent qualities allow for an explanation of the relation between our perceptions and the world which we perceive through them, by assigning different roles to different qualities and different statuses to the perceptions of these different qualities. Ideas of primary qualities have a direct connection to primary qualities that provide the most basic level of explanation, while secondary qualities are distinguished by our perceptions of ideas of secondary qualities. The assymetry is crucial: if there were no perceivers, what we call a secondary quality would merely be some of many unperceived ways of arranging primary qualities, since in considering secondary qualities we move from perceptions (ideas of secondary qualities) to things (secondary qualities) but vice versa with primary qualities. The distinction has great plausibility since it both separates perceptions more prone to perceptual variation[59] from those less prone, and uses the difference between the types of qualities for explanation.

Philonous begins to attack the distinction and undermine the foundational status of primary qualities with the example of a mite. Imagine perceiving the world through the eyes of a mite.[60] Like us, the mite has to make sense of the world. It uses its senses to seek pleasure and to avoid pain. Does the mite see its leg as having the microscopic magnitude that we see a mite's leg as having? Clearly

not, otherwise it would have great trouble avoiding many objects
that could cause it pain. The mite sees its mite leg relative to it, just
as we humans see our legs relative to us. If you accept that mites have
perceptions – which a Cartesian would not but a Lockean would[61] –
then perceptions of magnitude and extension are as relative to the
minds of perceivers as perceptions of colour and sound. The relative
character of measures has been an important theme in twentieth-
century philosophy of science,[62] and these and others of Berkeley's
arguments continue to be considered in different forms: for example,
the 'coastline paradox', which shows that the length of the coastline
of Britain depends on the size of the measuring stick and which led
to fractal geometry.[63]

Berkeley provides other thought experiments that also back his
point. Imagine looking at a slide under a microscope with one eye;
and imagine you can look at the same slide with the other eye unaided
by the microscope. You are perceiving the same slide at the same time,
the same object, and yet each eye perceives drastically different
magnitudes, shapes, colours, etc. The slide can't be both sizes at the
same time, therefore the differences in magnitude must be artefacts
of our perception. Both microscope and mite examples were standard early modern thought experiments, drawing on microscopy and
a world only accessible through the scientific instruments that had
been designed and theorized by the proponents of the new science.
Berkeley is turning the examples around and using them against a
crucial early modern distinction.[64] He uses similar arguments against
other primary qualities: motion (by showing the perceptual relativity
of judgments such as swift and slow), solidity, and figure.

A Lockean could certainly respond: 'I accept that there is something mind dependent about the ways in which we perceive these
qualities, but this does not mean: (1) that the qualities are wholly
mind dependent; and (2) that they are *as* susceptible to illusion as
primary qualities.' Berkeley has made his case mostly with visual
illusion, but it appears that when I touch something which is proximate I do know it's there in a way that I do not know magnitudes.
This is susceptible to illusion as well, but far less so. Berkeley's
response will be: 'I do not deny that our senses tell us something, I
deny that they tell us facts about a mind-independent world or that
there is a mind-independent world. They tell us things like "Ouch,
move".' The answer does not seem wholly satisfactory: why don't
they tell us 'This hot thing is out there burning me and I must move

my hand away from it!' as they appear to. Furthermore it raises the interesting question of the apparently intermediate status of our bodies between mind and world, which may pose a further problem for Berkeley.

These questions are related to Berkeley's use of a characteristically Lockean theme against the distinctions between qualities. Locke argued in the *Essay* that we can have no certain knowledge of the essences of things and bodies through physical science, unlike mathematics and morals (which we construct). This is not as tragic as we might at first think, since the ultimate purpose of natural science and philosophy is to aid us in our lives, and to make our lives happier in such a way as conduces to the discharge of our moral and religious duties. Locke's instrumental attitude towards science combined with his awareness of the limitations of scientific inquiry was the inheritance of Sir Francis Bacon,[65] and was shared by many other early modern thinkers. We can know what we need to know for what matters most.[66]

Like Locke, Berkeley held that our senses were not outfitted to take in eternal truths about an external world of things, but rather to navigate through this world in a manner that conduces to our benefit. In this context he makes an observation about the distinction between primary and secondary qualities:

> Heat and cold, tastes and smells, have something more vividly pleasing or disagreeable than the ideas of extension, figure, and Motion, affect us with. And it being too visibly absurd to hold, that pain or pleasure can be in an unperceiving substance, men are more easily weaned from believing the external existence of the secondary, than the primary qualities.

Since secondary qualities seem intuitively to be more proximate to pain and pleasure – in fact they are inseparable from vehement sensations – and since they are closely connected to our benefit (tasty croissant, alluring cologne, hot pits of hell), we naturally see them as connected to our desires and our minds. Ideas of other qualities are more remote from pain and pleasure: they are present so that we might ward off the things that threaten to cause us pain, and pursue those that give us pleasure (*NTV* 59), and so we presume them to be mind independent without thinking the issue through sufficiently.

A defender of the mind independence of primary qualities in general, and those qualities associated with space, extension, and distance (or depth) in particular, can respond that there are illusions in perceiving any and all qualities, but that these illusions can often be explained by reference to a standard (just as was the case with the variability of colour). So, variations in distance or depth can be explained due to properties of our sensory apparatus (tiny mite eyes), optical illusions, and what have you. That we experience illusions and that we do not take in distance and other qualities purely and immediately does not mean that there is not some absolute standard of distance distinct from our relative and perception-dependent experiences of distance. Furthermore, if extension – i.e. space and distance – is absolute, then we might use it to anchor the other primary qualities. We can say that although judgments of swift and slow are dependent on our perception, since there is absolute extension, the distance traversed over a set time can still be compared.

Characterizing space mathematically, and then using mathematics for scientific explanation was one of the great triumphs of early modern natural philosophy. Descartes' use of a coordinate system for geometrical objects then allowed him to characterize optics and vision geometrically. Berkeley's *New Theory of Vision* was an attack on Descartes-influenced theories of vision (such as Malebranche's) which argued that we see geometrical relations and then calculate to make sense of optical phenomena. Also, by abstractly characterizing space they tended to reduce width, breadth, up and down, and depth all to interchangeable dimensions: lines and grids in a co-ordinate system. We are all used to this: it's how we learn to represent objects as three-dimensional when we draw them. One of Berkeley's central insights in the *Notebooks* and the *New Theory of Vision* was that distance or depth was wholly different from width and breadth: they were not interchangeable, in a way which we will now consider.

In line with Descartes and Malebranche, Hylas tries to maintain a distinction between absolute extension and sensible extension (i.e., extension insofar as we sense it) against Philonous. This exchange seems particularly directed towards Newton, and has Berkeley putting one of the most celebrated Newtonian doctrines in Hylas' mouth. In the famed Scholium to the Definitions which began the *Philosophiae Naturalis Principia Mathematica* (1687), Newton claimed that absolute space was 'of its own nature', had no relation to anything external, and was always the same and immovable. Relative space, by contrast, was a movable measure of absolute space, determined by our senses in relation to our bodies or some other body. The problem, Newton admitted, was how to access absolute space:

> Since the parts of space cannot be seen, or distinguished from one another by our senses, we apply sensible measures to them. For we define all (*universa*) place from the positions and distances of things from a body that we consider immovable; and then we estimate all motions with respect to such places . . . And so, instead of absolute places and motions, we use relative ones; which makes for no inconveniences in common affairs; but in philosophical uses we ought to abstract from our senses (*in Philosophicis autem abstrahendum est a sensibus*), which we are able to do, for there may be no body really at rest, to which the places and motions refer.[67]

Quite strikingly, Newton is admitting that we can only access absolute space *through* relative space, that we can never see it, and that when we discuss absolute space philosophically we need to *abstract from our senses*. The paradigm example of accessing absolute space through relative space would be Newton's famous bucket experiment, where the concave surface of a rotating bucket shows us the phenomenal effects of absolute space (and the necessity of positing absolute space), since there is no relative explanation of the concavity of the surface in terms of the bucket (i.e. it does not move in relation to the bucket).

Since Newton himself had linked absolute space to philosophical abstraction, it is no surprise that Berkeley attacked the idea of absolute space as an abstract idea. He was also tacitly attacking the idea, espoused by Samuel Clarke (in his proof of God and in his correspondence with Leibniz) and by Newton, that God is connected to absolute space and that it functions as his instrument or *sensorium*. There is an intriguing theological backdrop for this difference: by positing an absolute, real abstract space, which is sensibly inaccessible, Newton's God becomes more remote and opposed to powerless creatures.[68] To be absolute, space must be abstracted from the particular things that occupy space, whether you hold that bodies are in space (as Newton did) or are modes of space (as Descartes and Spinoza did). On either count, to abstract space is to consider space independent from particular extended (or spatial) things. In Newton's case it is to consider absolute space through our acquaintance with particular extended (or spatial) things.

But abstracting from particular things causes an immediate problem for philosophers committed to the idea that to exist is just to be particular in some sense. Newton's friend Locke had claimed in his discussion of the 'Names of Substance' that 'every thing that exists, has its particular Constitution,' (*E* III.6.17), and Berkeley noted that this was in direct conflict with the notion of an uninstantiated, abstract space: if to be a thing means to have a particular constitution, then how can abstract space (i.e. space abstracted from every particular thing) be a thing?

Even if Locke's axiom is rejected, the abstract idea of absolute space still has the same problems as other abstract ideas. Philonous once again challenges Hylas to frame an abstract notion – here an absolute space devoid of any sensible qualities – and Hylas fails the challenge. Why? Philonous asks Hylas if he can even 'separate the ideas of extension and motion from the ideas of all those qualities which they who make the distinction, term secondary' (*D* 193).

This hints at a possible justification. The abstract idea of space must always involve particular ideas of touch. They are interconnected in images specific to each of the senses, and then associated through experience (for reasons that I will discuss in the next section) with vision and other senses. In the more extensive discussion of the impossibility of framing an abstract idea of space in the *Principles*, Berkeley adds:

> When therefore supposing all the world to be annihilated besides my own body, I say there still remains *pure space*: thereby nothing else is meant, but only that I conceive it possible, for the limbs of my body to be moved on all sides without the least resistance: but if that too were annihilated, then there would be no motion, and consequently no space. (*P* 116)

Consequently, when Berkeley says that it is impossible to separate the ideas of extension and motion from secondary qualities in the *Dialogues*, he seems to mean that our ideas of space always have built in the particular ways in which we acquire these ideas, and the content 'space' cannot be separated from touch in that they are not just a general content acquired through a sense but are instead always linked with the motion of *this* body. Berkeley's formulation here is strikingly similar to the so-called Master Argument, which I will consider in the concluding section.

Berkeley thought that Newton had been misled into positing absolute space due to his extraordinary ability to provide mathematical descriptions of natural phenomena. Since the mathematics lacks any reference to sensible modes, Newton then inferred that there must be a real insensible space being described mathematically. But the fact that they could be arranged mathematically said nothing as to the existence or even the conceivability of mathematical tools as metaphysical concepts and entities. The same could be said of Descartes, whom Berkeley is probably criticizing as well. On Descartes' account extension is identified with body, yet independent of the sensible modes by which we acquire our idea of extension.

The rejection of absolute space and absolute motion was one of Berkeley's central philosophical commitments. Eight years later, in *De Motu,* Berkeley argued that Newtonian absolute space was inconceivable, issuing a similar challenge to form an abstract idea of space (*DM* 54). As in the *Principles,* he argued that we smuggle a relative space with our own body at the centre into 'absolute space' when we believe we have formed an idea of 'absolute space' (while what we have actually formed is a threadbare, relative, ego-centred space). Judgments of distance or depth involved particular ideas of touch for Berkeley, and the way in which we felt other bodies and the way in which our body itself moves – one of his most intriguing and compelling ideas. This is primordial and impossible to erase from our experience, and it remains even when we believe that we are forming an absolutely abstract idea[69] – it is our lived space. After discussing substratum, I will return to the problem of space by considering Berkeley's arguments concerning distance.

Substratum, distance and depth (195–200, 201–3)

Confronted with all of these objections, Hylas is forced to reconsider much of what he had so recently gained through the distinctions between primary and secondary qualities. But he is still not prepared to give up a mind-independent world, and so he moves from arguing for a gap between the individual senses and what they perceive to distinguishing 'the *Object* from the *Sensation*' (*D* 194). (He might have wished to try this tactic a bit earlier, in that he has already conceded to Philonous a great deal about perception and what we perceive.) The distinction raises questions for Berkeley's account as well. What unifies the many particular perceptions of the different senses in such a way that we perceive tulips and snowballs as opposed to 'this red and that red and this smell and that smell, etc.'? What more generally is the relation between perceptions and what we perceive?

Initially, Hylas attempts to use the distinction between passive and active perception to argue that there are some aspects of perception that are passive, and since we take no active role in forming or undertaking these perceptions they must be mind independent or must represent something which is mind independent, i.e., an object distinct from but perceived by sensation. Philonous quickly undermines Hylas' arguments by noting that pain and colour are thoroughly mind dependent, but clearly also passive experiences in the sense that we have little control over them.

But Hylas also tries another more promising line of argument. In order for objects to exist, the modes and qualities that I perceive appear to need a material support or substratum that holds them up. Hylas is parroting Locke's famous assertion that we have an idea of 'a support of such Qualities, which are capable of producing simple Ideas in us' (*E* II.23.1). Locke admitted that the idea of substance was obscure[70] and confused, but at the same time presupposed in our thinking about objects. There are numerous interpretations of the Lockean doctrine of substance: as ultimately equivalent to what Locke called the 'real essence' or unknown but in principle scientifically accessible constitutions of individuals or natural kinds; or as logical subjects of predication; or as persistent and stable individuals. A substratum need not be material – on some of these interpretations of Locke it is not, and Aristotle, Descartes and countless others discuss spiritual or thinking substances – but Hylas immediately describes it as a 'material substratum'[71] and this makes clear both how Berkeley interpreted Locke's substances, and that this argument is a step towards immaterialism.

Berkeley attacked the idea of material substratum or substance by attacking the sense in which it supposedly stands under or supports qualities. We have a confused notion that a substance stands under qualities in the same way that our insides hold up our outsides, or our legs support our body, or a pizza is spread under and supports its toppings. If that is the case then substance must be extended. But then any substance will need another extended substance to support its extended qualities, and so on down. This argument is in fact from Locke, who introduces substance by asserting that:

> if he were demanded, what is it, that the Solidity and Extension inhere in, he would not be in a much better case, than the Indian before mentioned; who, saying that the World was supported by a great Elephant, was asked, what the Elephant rested on; to which his answer was, a great Tortoise; But being again pressed to know what gave support to the broad-back'd Tortoise, replied, something, he knew not what. (*E* II.23.2)

Locke develops a sophisticated response to this problem both in what follows this example in Book II of the *Essay* and in the later chapter 'On the Names of Substance' (*E* III.6), but it still poses a problem for Hylas, given that he has now accepted that the distinction between primary qualities and secondary qualities is not well-founded. Primary qualities, such as extension and solidity, need support: they are 'qualities of' just as much as and for the same reasons that secondary qualities are. Consequently, if support must be extended, extension needs its own extension.

Hylas has a number of avenues of response. First, although a Cartesian might identify a body with extension and view qualities as expressions of an underlying substance, Locke certainly didn't. If matter is anything for Locke it is corpuscles, and corpuscles can be characterized by a number of the primary qualities. Next, just because primary qualities and secondary qualities are all mind dependent (to some degree), it doesn't mean that they can't have different roles or functions. In fact it seems obvious that they do – extension is extension and colour is colour, and each can be characterized in a way that the other cannot. In taking over the philosophical vocabulary from his opponents, Berkeley identifies 'mode', 'accident', and 'quality', and 'modes' and 'accidents' are by definition 'modes of' and 'accidents of'. So although extension might provide support but not need support, and might just be the sort of quality that extension is, if it is also a mode (or an accident) it would seem to need something further to underlie it which it is 'of'. But there's no reason, given what has been argued up to this point, to interpret qualities in this way. In fact, Berkeley's normal use of quality just identifies them with immediate perceptual experience.

Of course, if one grants Berkeley's identification there's no need for material substances underlying anything!

Perhaps Berkeley thought that in attacking material substance at this point in the argument, he was attacking another version of the distinction between primary qualities and secondary qualities, where now one or two qualities (solidity and extension) perform a function different from the other qualities. If one quality performs this function, and if all qualities need to have the function performed since they are matter, and so passive, then what will then perform this function for the lonely quality which performs for the others? Consequently philosophers should reject the identification of substance and support, which seems the other goal of the argument. We shouldn't expect the argument to show that matter doesn't exist, since Berkeley has further arguments for that! At most it can show that matter does not exist in a certain way – as a substance.

There is a different problem that concerns the use that Berkeley will make of substances in the 'Third Dialogue'. There he assumes that spirits or minds are substances, and that the notion of mental substance is unproblematic in a way that material substance is not. If the problems with material substance are problems with substance as such, and if this holds for minds, then Berkeley's use of mental substance has little support (so to speak). I do not think the passages in the *Dialogues* we have just examined point to a problem in the concept of substance, but rather that a substance might be material.[72] Matter always needs something to support or underlie it because it is passive, whereas spirits are active and can underlie without needing further underlaying.

In the 'Third Dialogue' Berkeley remarks:

> In the very Notion or Definition of material Substance, there is included a manifest Repugnance and Inconsistency. But this cannot be said of the Notion of Spirit. That Ideas should exist in what doth not perceive, or be produced by what doth not act, is repugnant. (*D* II: 233)

For the moment it is clear that the problems lie not in substance but in something that is perceived existing in something that does not perceive, or something that is thought, and indeed just is how and that it is thought, in something that is unthinking. How can something that is unthinking have thoughts in it? This is not a problem for spirits or minds or divine substance.

Later in the 'First Dialogue' Berkeley returns to the theme of extended magnitude and considers distance. Hylas is again trying to establish that there is an object beyond our perceptions, and the sense of sight and visual experience of distance seem to have 'outside' and 'external' built into them. He mentions the examples of the stars, which seem external to me, and I judge them as external because they are very distant. When I say 'Alexander Hamilton is now ten paces from me', I assume that Hamilton is an object external to me and that I perceive his distance – ten paces. Berkeley's emphasis on distance as arising from touch not vision, which I have mentioned in the previous section, is central to his arguments in the *New Theory of Vision* for the mind dependence of visual distance. In fact, Berkeley added a footnote referring to the *New Theory of Vision* (and in the later edition of the *Dialogues* to the *New Theory of Vision Vindicated*) to these passages of the *Dialogues*, so he clearly wanted readers to look there to buttress his arguments.

It seems counterintuitive to say that we do not see distance, but consider one of Berkeley's favourite examples. When we look at an object at a great distance, how do we know it's at a great distance? Our eyes strain and we cannot make out what is at a distance as clearly as what is near – so we 'see' the object *as distant* based on different visual clues. We presume that visual clues naturally signify various, different distances, and in this sense we see distance. But now consider someone who is nearsighted and has no glasses (or just take off your own if you wear glasses). The nearsighted person's eyes strain, they have the same clues as the person with ordinary vision, but they do not conclude that the object they are trying to see is at a distance (*NTV* 37). As with the inference from blush to shame we considered when we discussed the difference between artificial and natural signs, this is also an example of what at first appears to be a natural sign turning out to be a series of conventional associations – different for the nearsighted person and the person with 20/20 vision. Consequently we do not see distance, we associate sensations of touch with relations in our depthless visual field. Philosophers like Descartes and Newton who presume a uniform conception of space are in fact drawing on two heterogeneous sources of ideas – touch and sight.

In the *Dialogues*, Berkeley alludes to a few of the specific arguments from the *New Theory Vision* (of which there are many more).[73] These include one of his favourite arguments: that if distance is supposed to be a line from the eye to the object, we cannot see distance since it would have to be turned endwise to the eye! He (very) quickly mentions Molyneux's problem (not by name) and states that the blind man when given sight would not have any sense of distance 'annexed' to his visual perceptions but would 'take them to be a new set of sensations existing only in his mind' (*D* II: 202). This is an intriguing thought on Berkeley's part, borne out to some extent by research on stimulating the visual cortex in the blind, that initial vision would be disorganized *minima visibilia*, and that only with time would the swimming visual mess become sufficiently organized to be 'distant' or 'round' or 'lovely' or 'external'. Only when they had been annexed to touch, and particularly to the experience of seeking pleasures of touch and avoiding pains, would they then come to signify heuristics for avoiding bad feelings – distance.

Hylas puts up little resistance because Locke had, like Berkeley, answered 'Not' to Molyneux's question, but without drawing this consequence (*E* II.9.8). Berkeley then reminds Hylas that since colours seem to be on objects, and appear to be at a distance (but cannot be, since they are in the mind), judgments that something is distant are questionable. This argument is much weaker, in that Hylas is open to respond that it is not the colours that appear distant but what is coloured: but Hylas is cowed!

The main point that Berkeley is trying to hammer home is that our senses do not deceive us, but we deceive ourselves as to what can properly be inferred from them. We falsely believe that our senses must naturally tell us what is in fact only the consequence of convention and association. Philonous remarks:

> The idea or thing which you immediately perceive, neither sense nor reason inform you that it actually exists without the mind. By sense you only know that you are affected with such certain sensations of light and colours, &c. And these you will not say without the mind. (*D* II: 201)

This was one of the central lessons of early modern theories of perception and knowledge: do not make unwarranted inferences on the basis of apparently obvious sense experience. Berkeley is making this point in a more systematic and thoroughgoing way against its advocates: for example, Descartes' theory of vision, which took distance to be an intellectual inference based on the perception of primary qualities, or the presumptions built into Newtonian absolute space.

The 'Master Argument', double existence, and the bell tolls for Hylas (200–1, 203–7)

Berkeley's arguments against corporeal or material substratum are not completely satisfying, and thankfully Philonous concludes not with 'material substratum does not exist' or even 'matter does not exist' but instead that Hylas – whose name means matter – really knows nothing about matter. Philonous adds that belief in a substratum implies that 'when you conceive the real existence of qualities, you do withal conceive something which you cannot conceive' (*D* II: 199). Berkeley is suggesting that the inconceivability follows from two contradictory assertions: (1) that 'real', explanatorily prior causes of or underlying supports for sense perceptions *are not* perceived immediately by the senses; and (2) that all sense perceptions *are* immediately perceived by the senses. The contradiction requires a further premise: that the real qualities must have an essential property in common with the perceptions which they cause in order to function as causes or supports. This premise seems to be assumed by Locke when he wrote 'the *Ideas of primary Qualities* of Bodies, *are Resemblances* of them, and their Patterns do really exist in the Bodies themselves' (*E* II.8.15).

That a cause must have something in common with the effect, or that a support must have something in common with the qualities it supports, was a commonplace for seventeenth- and eighteenth-century philosophers. Berkeley was combining this premise with the admitted mind dependence of some qualities to then try to argue that mind-dependent ideas could not have mind-independent things which are not ideas as their causes. Berkeley's argument depends on moving step by step through the many proposed real causes of ideas, and showing each to be unsatisfactory. One has a sneaking suspicion, however, that arguments like the microscope argument have shown not that qualities are wholly mind dependent, but that they are at least somewhat mind dependent.

Hylas draws on this suspicion with the objection:

> Now, I grant that each quality cannot singly subsist without the mind. colour cannot without extension, neither can figure without some other sensible quality. But as the several qualities united or blended together form entire sensible things, nothing

hinders why such things may not be supposed to exist without the mind.

Berkeley's procedure has shown that each quality in isolation from other qualities is not independent of the mind. But just as the qualities when taken together form one thing differentiable from the particular sensible qualities experienced, so too couldn't the qualities combine in such a way as to result in mind-independent things?

This is a serious question, since it draws on the unity of our perceptions of things to argue that mind independence might emerge from combination, and thus sets the tone for the concluding sections of the 'First Dialogue'. Philonous immediately responds that the arguments have shown that secondary qualities are 'not *at all* without the mind . . . because it was impossible even in thought to separate them from all secondary qualities, so as to conceive them existing by themselves.' In other words, since we cannot conceive of primary qualities as separable from other qualities, we perceive through a particular sense. Notably, this is the same formula that Berkeley invoked in his discussion of absolute and relative space.

But what does this really show? Two types of properties cannot be abstracted from one another, cannot be conceived separately. If primary and secondary qualities are as connected as Berkeley suggests (i.e., as in the example we considered previously of the acquisition of ideas of space), then the distinction between the qualities is itself questionable, much like the distinction between pain and vehement heat. We would need to view qualities as different aspects or ways of perceiving complex images particular to each sense. Furthermore, on this account primary qualities could no longer be considered as acquired by multiple senses.

This discussion initiates Berkeley's most infamous argument, often called 'The Master Argument',[74] and should be kept firmly in mind when considering it. It is very brisk argument, given the conclusion it purports to demonstrate:

> Philonous: I am content to put the whole upon this issue. If you can conceive it possible for any mixture or combination of qualities, or any sensible object whatever, to exist without the Mind, then I will grant it actually to be so.
> Hylas: If it comes to that, the point will soon be decided. What

more easy than to conceive a tree or house existing by itself, independent of, and unperceived by any mind whatsoever? I do at this
present time conceive them existing after that manner.

Philonous: How say you, Hylas, can you see a thing which is at
the same time unseen?

Hylas: No, that were a contradiction.

Philonous: Is it not as great a contradiction to talk of *conceiving*
a thing which is *unconceived*?

Hylas: It is.

Philonous: The tree or house therefore which you think of, is conceived by you.

Hylas: How should it be otherwise?

Philonous: And what is conceived, is surely in the mind.

Hylas: Without question, that which is conceived is in the
Mind.

Philonous: How then came you to say, you conceived a house
or tree existing independent and out of all minds whatsoever? (*D*
II: 200)

This argument is also in the *Principles* in a slightly different form
(and a somewhat different context):

But, say you, surely there is nothing easier than for me to imagine
trees, for instance, in a park, or books existing in a closet, and
nobody by to perceive them. I answer, you may so, there is no
difficulty in it; but what is all this, I beseech you, more than
framing in your mind certain ideas which you call books and
trees, and the same time omitting to frame the idea of any one
that may perceive them? But do not you yourself perceive or
think of them all the while? This therefore is nothing to the
purpose; it only shews you have the power of imagining or
forming ideas in your mind: but it does not shew that you can
conceive it possible the objects of your thought may exist
without the mind. To make out this, it is necessary that you conceive them existing unconceived or unthought of, which is a
manifest repugnancy. When we do our utmost to conceive the
existence of external bodies, we are all the while only contem-
plating our own ideas. But the mind taking no notice of itself, is
deluded to think it can and does conceive bodies existing
unthought of or without the mind, though at the same time they

are apprehended by or exist in itself. A little attention will discover to any one the truth and evidence of what is here said, and
make it unnecessary to insist on any other proofs against the existence of material substance. (*P* 23)

The argument is best known through the *Principles* version, but very
few philosophers have been convinced by either version. This is the
argument that David Stove dismissively referred to as 'the Gem'.
There are many reasons not to be convinced.

First, Berkeley moves from perceive to conceive, and conflates the
two verbs without any explanation. I can in principle conceive of
many things that I have not perceived (for example, how a mite might
perceive the world), and there are many aspects of things that I perceive but cannot conceive (I perceive that a microscope really works
but I cannot conceive how a microscope really works).

Next, as was objected against Berkeley's argument against the
conceivability of abstract ideas, just because Hylas cannot conceive
of a tree which he has not conceived does not mean that there is no
tree, or that it is inconceivable! Furthermore, even if there can be no
tree which I do not perceive, that doesn't mean that there might not
be something out there which I do not have the slightest acquaintance with, which I have never attempted to conceive because I have
no concept for it at all.

The argument is too strong in another direction as well. If to conceive of an object is always to conceive of mind-dependent qualities
– i.e., to conceive of qualities in one's own mind – then we only ever
conceive of our own minds. This would seem to commit Berkeley to
a gross solipsism that he would wish to avoid.

Furthermore, Berkeley seems to be confusing *thinking about* a tree
with *thinking that there is* a tree which has the property of being
unperceived. The two are clearly not the same in that the former
implies that I can (at least in principle) describe the tree (the tree I
saw last Wednesday in my Grandmother's yard . . . you know, the
big, green one), whereas the latter does not (a tree in a forest). These
are not all the objections; there are legions more! But this is enough
to work with to get a sense of what the argument is meant to show,
and what it is probably not meant to show.

In each of the two versions of the argument, Berkeley uses one
of the standard formulas with which he issued his challenges for
abstract ideas – 'If you can conceive', 'frame the idea' – which

further hints that there may be a connection between the Master Argument and his criticisms of abstract ideas. Indeed, Berkeley remarked early in the *Principles*:

> what do we perceive besides our own ideas or sensations? and is it not plainly repugnant that any one of these, or any combination of them, should exist unperceived? If we thoroughly examine this tenet it will, perhaps, be found at bottom to depend on the doctrine of abstract ideas. For can there be a nicer strain of abstraction than to distinguish the existence of sensible objects from their being perceived, so as to conceive them existing unperceived? (*P* 4–5)

It is less apparent how abstraction is involved in the *Dialogues* version, but as I noted there are clues in the text that it is. The *Principles* version of the argument seems to draw on the claim that you cannot perceive and not have it be *your* perception in your mind with *you* perceiving – i.e., that the content of the perception ('this green') cannot be separated from the egocentric, perspectival character of its acquisition. There is always an 'I' in the picture who must be there to do the perceiving, just in the sense that all the perceptions have one of us at their centre. What is being abstracted on this account is some property or quality of the idea acquired through perception which is wholly independent of the way it was acquired – a View from Nowhere in an arena where to be a View is to be a View by Someone. If the sensible object is sensible it has to be sensed, and if it is sensed it is sensed by someone from somewhere, and so forth. Berkeley seems to be developing an account of what it is to perceive and arguing that if you accept this account then you accept immaterialism.

Note that as against the objection that Berkeley's argument is too strong and implies solipsism, this only goes through if by mind dependent is understood *exclusively, in the mind that perceives it*. But this is in fact not implied by the argument. It must be in my mind if I am to perceive it, but that doesn't mean that it couldn't be in another intending mind as well – two minds might share a perspective. Whether this implies a Vulcan mind-meld or an all-perceiving God with access to my thoughts and those of others will need to be discussed later!

In the *Dialogues* version of the argument, Philonous begins with the apparently uncontroversial supposition that the answer to '*can you* see a thing which is *at the same time* [my emphasis] unseen' is: 'No, that were a contradiction'. There are two significant ambiguities in Philonous' question, which I have just alluded to. First, 'can you' could be construed as (1) 'is it possible for one to'; or (2) 'are *you* Hylas able to'; or (3) 'can one (Hylas, or someone else)'. Berkeley could be fallaciously trading on this ambiguity in trying to establish that something is impossible as such due to the fact that just Hylas cannot do something. The modifier 'at the same time' is also ambiguous, and could mean either 'also has the property for the duration of time we are looking at the object', or just 'also has the property'. The duration reading allows that we could see something that is now seen and unseen at a different time, whereas the property reading might entail that we could never see an object if this object had the property 'unseen'.

Hylas agrees that it is a contradiction, but why? On any reading, the thing would both have the property 'seen' and 'unseen', and since 'unseen' is 'not seen' it seems fairly straightforward. This is a standard argument of Berkeley's ,which we have seen before. Still, if I see a tree, and you don't, it is both seen and unseen, and that certainly doesn't seem to be contradictory. It is necessary to stipulate who sees and unsees, in fact that at least one perceiver does so. The most natural way to construe Philonous' query is: 'Are you Hylas able to see a thing which is at the same time unseen by anyone at all including you Hylas?' 'No', seems about right.

Berkeley moves from this moderately controversial claim to a far more controversial one: 'Is it not as great a contradiction to talk of conceiving a thing which is unconceived?' Most philosophers would answer 'No, in fact it is not'; but Hylas answers 'It is'. As I remarked before, Berkeley moves without comment from 'see' to 'conceive' with nary an explanation or even idling at 'perceived'. This might be explained on his behalf. Conceiving of, or having a concept of some thing which is perceived through the senses – such as a tree or a house – must follow from having actually associated diverse immediate sense perceptions. A concept, as opposed to a percept, is general and publicly accessible. In Berkeleyan terms it is a word and a cluster of ideas, or what Berkeley calls a 'general idea' as opposed to an abstract idea. To have a general idea or a sense concept is just to have ideas or images particular to each of the senses, and to organize and selectively attend to these images and to revive them through memory.

The restriction is neutral (for the moment) as to whether there might be concepts or notions (Berkeley's term) which are not ideas, or derived from sense perceptions, and to which the argument does not apply (like of an insensible God, or quantum phenomena). But, when Berkeley says that we cannot conceive something unconceived, and that this is manifestly repugnant, he must mean that we cannot conceive of something which is immediately perceived by the senses – such as a tree – if it is not derived from immediate, perspectival sense perceptions.

As I noted, the passages directly preceding the Master Argument tend to support this reading, since they stress that primary and secondary qualities are not separable. Berkeley's challenge of 'Is it not as great a contradiction to talk of conceiving a thing which is unconceived?' could then be rephrased: 'It is contradictory to conceive a sense object which has no connection to sense perception for reasons connected to my rejection of abstraction and the ultimately perspectival character of all perceptions, since visual and tactile qualities are ultimately ways of considering images which are in turn ego-centred seeings and touchings.' This is considerably more modest, and draws on far more presuppositions than the actual argument appears to be at first. The *Dialogue* form allows for quick arguments, the support for which has been built by what precedes (and in this case the *New Theory of Vision* as well).

If this is the case then Berkeley's argument would also deny that we can think about something sense perceivable without some connection to thinking that something is the case. If it is objected that it would be open to Hylas to maintain that, though he may not be able to conceive of trees existing independent of the mind, this is compatible with him thinking that there are such, Berkeley can answer that the objection is closed on the grounds that he rejects a theory of concepts or abstract ideas that separates the two.

These are the more controversial issues: Does Berkeley draw on different senses of quality, on ambiguities between unperceived and unperceivable? Admittedly Berkeley was too excited by his clever conceived/unconceived formulation, and swayed by the curtain of words perhaps he thought he had a stronger argument than maybe he really did! But certainly what Stove wants to take from the argument as the Gem – that 'you cannot have trees-without-the-mind in mind, without having them in mind. Therefore, you cannot have trees-without-the-mind in mind' – needs context to make sense of why Berkeley thought it to hold.

One very strange, but also revealing criticism was made by Hume. In the discussion of 'Scepticism of the senses' in *A Treatise*, Hume claimed that the mind is just a bundle of perceptions, and that each of the bundled perceptions is in principle separable. If a perception can be separated from all the others, then it would be an 'unperceived perception' (*T* IV.3.33). This is of course not what Berkeley meant, but it raises the interesting issue of whether the Master Argument assumes a unified perceiver with unified acts of thought.[75]

A final (for now, there's one more at the end of the chapter) objection has been offered by George Pitcher, who distinguishes between 'what is conceived of' and 'what is conceived with'.[76] What is conceived *of* in the Master Argument is a tree. What is conceived *with* are sense experiences. The sense experiences represent the tree to us, but that doesn't mean the sense experiences *are* the tree. In fact, unless I can have different sense experiences of the same tree I will be plunged into the worst sort of sceptical nightmare, where there is nothing to unify my sense perceptions at all. This was a consequence that Hume drew in 'Scepticism of the Senses'. If we wish to avoid this consequence we should reject the Master Argument, as one of its basic premises is that what is conceived of *is* what is conceived with, and vice versa.

Berkeley's response to this sort of objection, or what of this objection he could formulate given that it depends on much later distinctions such as sense and reference, will come in the dialogues which follow. But that he wishes to reject the idea of an external object of any sort to which perceptions refers is apparent in his criticism of what might be called 'a double existence' hypothesis (following Hume): that things are known through ideas and that they have a separate existence from which the idea derives whatever is distinctive to it. Double existence has been tacitly assumed in many of Hylas' arguments: that real sounds are motions distinct from the sounds we hear, that absolute space underlies the sensible space which we experience, that real objects are distinct from the qualities we perceive. Philonous, and Berkeley, are attempting to draw together many of these previous arguments and show how they all draw upon a misconceived picture. In the double existence hypothesis, mind-dependent ideas represent mind-independent entities: they are 'copies, images or, representations of certain originals' (*D* II: 205). When I look at a bust of Julius Caesar the bust represents and resembles the historical Julius Caesar who is not perceived.

This assumption is also behind Locke's famous account of resemblance of primary qualities 'that the *Ideas of primary Qualities* of Bodies, *are Resemblances* of them, and their Patterns do really exist in the Bodies themselves' (*E* II.8.15). Ideas of primary qualities are natural signs of primary qualities, naturally represent them and are copies of them. What they represent does really exist, beyond the idea and is signified and represented by it.

Hylas is forced to bring this thesis up explicitly because his many other avenues of argument have been denied. Philonous adopts a two-pronged strategy much as he did with abstract ideas, arguing for impossibility and then providing an alternative explanation. First, what does Philonous think is wrong here? He asks us to imagine a man who knows nothing about Julius Caesar. When he looks at the representation what does this man see? 'Colours and figures with a certain symmetry and composition of the whole.' It is in fact not a natural sign but a conventional association.

It might be properly responded that even if the association is conventional: (1) That doesn't mean that it still doesn't represent Julius Caesar; and (2) there may be stronger examples than historical figures! Even taking both objections into account, Philonous has still secured what he wished to. For, if we are dealing with an arbitrary sign, it will need to be explained at each turn why and how it signifies and yet resembles something which is external. In each case an alternative explanation can be offered through association of heterogeneous sense perceptions that might be associated differently. Philonous follows his discussion of the coach, which we have considered previously, with the example of a hot iron bar:

> when we are said to see a red-hot bar of iron; the solidity and heat of the iron are not the objects of sight, but suggested to the imagination by the colour and figure, which are properly perceived by that sense. In short, those things alone are actually and strictly perceived by any sense, which would have been perceived, in case that same Sense had then been first conferred on us. As for other things, it is plain they are only suggested to the mind by experience grounded on former perceptions. (*D* II: 204)

Eventually we terminate the search for natural signification with each sense and its heterogeneous perceptions (or, if we are suspicious of the category of sense, with heterogeneous perceptions). We cannot infer from one sense to another except through association, and we certainly can't presume that sense experience testifies in a unified manner to a unifying external object, which is insensible and which it patterns itself after. What would it even mean in Berkeley's terms for 'this red', 'this hot' and 'this solid' to all be patterns of the same thing? Berkeley considers these sorts of objections – that sense experience is diverse, intermixed, irreducible to functionally and explanatorily distinguished classes of qualities, and wholly different from the stable, unperceived matter which it is supposed to represent – as fatal to the account. Hylas seeks stability for our perceptions, and the only sort of stability he can think of is matter. This is a good example of how, for Berkeley, the quest for external, material anchors pulls us away from God as an explanation – and this is the issue overarching all of these particular discussions.

Philonous suggests that we might need recourse to some sort of faculty beyond our senses to access these 'archetypes of our ideas . . . not perceived by sense': an 'internal faculty of the soul' like 'Reason or memory' (*D* II: 204). Hylas takes Philonous' suggestion that we might have *a priori* rational or innate access to the archetypes of things as mockery, and rules it out *tout à fait*. This suggests that Berkeley is not interested in attacking these sorts of positions, as neither Locke nor Malebranche defended innate access to external objects. But, at the same time, Berkeley introduces his important concept of archetype. If 'our ideas are continually changing upon every alteration in the distance, medium, or instruments of sensation', then what will give stability to our sense experience? On the one hand it seems that it must have stability; on the other hand it seems that it can't.

Philonous gloats a bit in triumph. He and Hylas had agreed that the greater sceptic 'denies the reality of sensible things, or professes the greatest Ignorance of them' and Hylas has now been show to be a sceptic through the consequences of two doctrines – that only ideas are like ideas and that no idea can exist without the mind. That Berkeley has not really shown the first of these satisfactorily goes unmentioned! Perhaps he takes this as a shared assumption of Cartesians (who did certainly hold it) and Lockeans (who may not).

Philonous senses that he has Hylas on the ropes and begins to press immaterialism, but the bell rings and the dialogue ends. Despite the flurry of argument at the end of the 'First Dialogue' this is in fact not a bell ringing the rounds of a boxing match, but a college bell which 'rings for prayers', and we now realize that the discussion has taken place in a college. They agree to meet again in the morning, and Hylas will try to conjure better arguments in the interim.

Questions

1. Do Berkeley's conclusions about the distinction between primary and secondary qualities tend to destroy all distinctions between qualities? Is this tenable?

2. Why does Berkeley think that vehement heat and pain are inseparable? Does it rest on a further thesis about what sorts of things populate the world and on what it is to be a thing?

3. Does Berkeley make a mistake of the following sort in the 'Master Argument', unwarrantedly moving from a true statement 'it is not possible to hold that the tree exists and is conceived and that the tree exists and is unconveived' to a questionable conclusion 'the tree exists and is conceived and it is not possible for a tree to exist and be unconceived'?[77]

THE 'SECOND DIALOGUE' (II: 207–26)

Nature and brain (207–10)

Hylas is once again late to meet Philonous. He excuses his tardiness to Philonous as due to the fact that his head was so filled with their previous discussion that he could not tell the time of day! Philonous had offered a strong challenge to Hylas at the end of the 'First Dialogue' to try to find any flaws in his reasoning. As the 'Second Dialogue' begins, Hylas sadly admits that the arguments offered by Philonous are 'clear and evident; the more I consider them, the more irresistibly do they force my assent'. These formulae – 'clear and evident' and 'force my assent' – would have been associated by his readers with Descartes, Hobbes, and Spinoza. All of these philosophers claimed that their philosophical methods forced assent in the reader.

Hobbes and Spinoza advocated geometrical methods, patterned after Euclid's *Elements*, which derived propositions from axioms and definitions. If a reader assented to the definitions and the axioms, and if they agreed that the proofs of the propositions drawing on these axioms and definitions were secure, then they were forced to assent to the conclusions. If the conclusions to which the reader was led were far from their prior beliefs, so much the worse for the prior beliefs.[78]

Descartes adopted a geometrical-style method in his *Principles*, but presented his *Meditations* in an internally critical and dialectical form, which he called an 'analytic' method.[79] The analytic method was to follow the natural order of thought with minimal presuppositions. The method should not be circumscribed by syllogisms, set topics, or the unjustified definitions and axioms from which a synthetic method takes its starting point. Rather, topics should arise naturally when they are appropriate, and definitions should be achievements and not starting points. Much like a dialogue, everything ought to be open to questioning: the inquiry should be as free from presupposition as possible and reflect natural human reason (as opposed to formal syllogisms, deductions and topics). Unlike a dialogue, the analytic method has the inquirer investigate and clear out his or her own mind, not through discussing with others, but instead through a kind of journey into the self – a meditation as journey into the self.

Both of these modern methods – analytic or Euclidean/synthetic – tended to promote beliefs far afield from common sense such as materialism (Hobbes), panpsychism (Spinoza), and non-interactive dualism (Descartes). One advantage of dialogue for Berkeley is that, in addition to 'forcing assent' through the interrogation of concepts, arguments and beliefs, it is also capable of returning readers to the world and to common sense through descriptions of the scene and the natural give and take of human interaction. This in turn checks the wildest excesses of metaphysical speculations, the sorts of argument one might hatch alone or with another wild-eyed metaphysician in one's closet.[80] This is of course not true of all dialogue (as we've seen with the examples from Malebranche and Fontenelle): but it is a tendency in dialogue which Berkeley exploits. Hylas leaves Philonous, gets agitated when alone, and then returns to become soothed by discussion in the college garden. This pattern plays itself out in the 'Third Dialogue' as well. Of course, Berkeley is equating immaterialism with common sense!

Berkeley wanted his readers both to assent to the consequences that his arguments justified and to come to recognize that what they assented to *was* common sense, even if it initially seemed at a great distance from ordinary beliefs. This marks a great divergence from someone like Spinoza, who viewed philosophers as capable of accessing rare and difficult ideas that the vulgar or common people could not. As discussed before, Berkeley thought that this kind of philosophical hubris led to atheism and immorality. In particular, philosophical arguments justified a picture of the world which was disconnected from our natural religious and moral beliefs. It proposed an account of what was 'natural' – a materialism built on presumptions about what sense perceptions and abstract concepts naturally signified – that in the end was horribly unnatural and far removed from our natural beliefs.[81]

Hylas still cannot rid himself of the idea that 'natural' must refer to an external, mechanistic and general cause, as opposed to the immaterialist position to which his natural reason naturally leads him. And so he tries throughout the 'Second Dialogue' to hold on to modern materialism within the constraints to which Philonous has forced him to assent. Berkeley understands that to disambiguate 'natural' from 'extended matter' has notable consequences for understanding what a natural sign is and how it is natural.

Hylas first attempts to smuggle matter back into the Berkeleyan picture by claiming that it is 'natural' to explain the senses through the brain, and that this is where natural reason leads us. And indeed, it probably seems even more natural to us to explain the senses with brain states or neural nets, or regions of brain activity, then it did to Berkeley's contemporaries. The picture of brain activity that Hylas offers is relatively primitive: nerves as strings and pulleys communicating impressions to the 'Seat of the Soul'. But the idea that mental events or sense perceptions are connected with or caused by brain events or brain processes is shared by both Berkeley's contemporaries and our own.

Philonous' criticism of the brain as the source of ideas of sensation goes along the lines that the reader has grown to expect. The repetition of arguments is doubtless conscious on Berkeley's part, an attempt to have readers begin to formulate the arguments and thus enter into the dialogue. The argument goes: (1) We experience and consequently know of the brain as a sensible thing, i.e., as organized, persistent, stable sense impressions from different senses (although hopefully more from sight than from smell, touch, hearing and taste!). (2) If this is the case then the ideas of the brain are, like all ideas, in the mind. (3) Then the brain is *in* the mind. (4) But if it is in the mind, it cannot cause or occasion the mind. To 'talk of ideas imprinted in an idea, causing that same idea, which is absurd' (*D* II: 209).

The argument rests on us accepting a premise that we have found controversial throughout the discussion of the 'First Dialogue', that to be an idea necessarily means to wholly be in the mind and to be nowhere else. This premise is presumed in (2). Steps (1) and (4) are also questionable. Do we really know the brain just through the senses? Couldn't we deny that the mind is caused by the brain and suggest that instead sense perceptions just are brain, i.e., that there is only identity between our sense experiences and material states or causally connected corpuscles? This was Spinoza's position (who was not a straightforward materialist), and is a position also open to the thoroughgoing materialist: our sense experience is not caused by brain states or processes or reducible to them, but rather is brain states. Indeed, Spinoza's argument against Descartes' attempts to locate the interaction between the extended substances and thinking substances in a common sense/ pineal gland is very similar to Berkeley's arguments against matter causing ideas.[82]

One could go further, and argue not just for identity but for what contemporary philosophers refer to as 'eliminativist' materialism. Berkeley's criticisms of the ways in which philosophers influence how we look at the world – that we are bewitched by half-mad philosophical assumptions about what the world is like, built on words purporting to represent abstract ideas – could just as easily be turned against Berkeley. Is there a good reason to presume that our ideas about how we ordinarily perceive are any more accurate than philosophical fantasy? Take the example I mention previously from Wilfrid Sellars about the tie store. Doesn't the example show that what it is to be 'green', a simple, purportedly pre-theoretical perception, presumes all sorts of context (outdoor lighting) and assumptions? Couldn't they be eliminated just in the way that our belief that distance is intrinsically visual was in the *New Theory of Vision*? We previously, briefly, considered that vehement sensations may be separable from pain. If this is the case then a simple perception such as the perception of 'pain' that begins Berkeley's inquiry may not be as straightforward as we think, and may be open to question. We might consequently begin to question our 'ordinary' perceptions.[83]

A Berkeleyan would likely respond that be this as it may, it is still the case that we access the material things that are said to cause our perceptions wholly through our perceptions. There is something ineliminable about the qualitative character of our sense experience, and it is through this experience that we know whatever else we know. This follows from Berkeley's methodological empiricism taken from Locke, that sense perception and reflection are the only sources of experience, perception and knowledge. Even if we can come to revise our common sense perceptions (and Berkeley holds that we clarify our common sense when we lift the 'curtain of words'), we do it by virtue of and through our ideas of sense perceptions, which are, well, ideas and not matter. It certainly does not warrant using 'matter' as an independent external cause of ideas of sense, which has been ruled out on the basis of any number of arguments that hold independent of the potential faultiness of common sense experiences.

Philonous instead eliminates matter – 'While accounting for ideas, by certain motions or impressions in the brain, that is, by some alterations in an idea, whether sensible or imaginable, it matters not'; and Hylas recants his hypothesis, admitting with a flourish worthy of Descartes that his argument that the brain causes sense perceptions was 'a mere Dream'. In this context Philonous introduces another important Berkeleyan concept in passing: 'Besides spirits, all that we know or conceive are our own ideas' (D II: 209). Berkeley is here suggesting that there are things that we can know beyond our own ideas: other spirits and our knowledge of them is not of ideas (which Berkeley equates with images). But this suggestion immediately raises an issue we have been avoiding – if so far all we know are our ideas and there is no external world of matter, how can we have access to other minds at all?

This was a central issue in Descartes' 'Sixth Meditation'. How do we know, for example, that the people we meet on the street really have minds at all, and aren't just machines beneath their clothes? Isn't that all we really perceive about them? Descartes' answer, that God is not a deceiver, was not very satisfying to many readers of the *Meditations*, since we are apparently deceived all of the time in our perceptions. Berkeley obviously doesn't have to deal with this particular sort of worry in one sense, since he denies matter. But he still must explain how and that we know other minds beyond our ideas.

Nature and feeling (210–11)

When Hylas first met up with Philonous at the opening of the 'First Dialogue', Philonous briefly described to him the sensible beauties of the garden. Now Philonous again describes the beauty of nature in specific terms, but in a somewhat different matter. He begins by asking Hylas whether now that he has been forced to recognize 'no sensible things have a real existence' he is 'in truth an arrant sceptic?' Hylas, having failed to show that the brain could function as a cause of sensation, is now saddled with the troubling thought that he has embraced scepticism in denying the existence of an external world. If there is no world beyond the mind, what is left besides our minds and ideas? The world seems to have become ghostly, inhabited only by floating, virtual spectres.

This is a key issue for Berkeley, given that he is advocating a kind of idealism. He does not, of course, wish dualists or materialists to dictate the terms of his idealism. And just because one is an idealist doesn't mean that 'ideas' must be thin[84] representatives of the external world *sans* external world. But the question is: What then? Philonous' long response is worth quoting at length, because it begins to answer this question:

> Look! are not the fields covered with a delightful verdure? Is there not something in the woods and groves, in the rivers and clear springs that sooths, that delights, that transports the soul? At the prospect of the wide and deep ocean, or some huge mountain whose top is lost in the clouds, or of an old gloomy forest, are not our minds filled with a pleasing horror? Even in rocks and deserts, is there not an agreeable wildness? How sincere a pleasure is it to behold the natural beauties of the earth! To preserve and renew our relish for them, is not the veil of night alternately drawn over her face, and doth she not change her dress with the seasons? How aptly are the elements disposed? What variety and use in the meanest productions of Nature? What delicacy, what beauty, what contrivance in animal and vegetable bodies? How exquisitely are all things suited, as well to their particular ends, as to constitute apposite parts of the whole! And while they mutually aid and support, do they not also set off and illustrate each other? . . . How vivid and radiant is the lustre of the fixed stars! How magnificent and rich that negligent profusion, with which they appear to be scattered throughout the whole azure

vault! Yet if you take the telescope, it brings into your sight a new host of stars that escape the naked eye. Here they seem contiguous and minute, but to a nearer view immense orbs of light at various distances, far sunk in the abyss of space. Now you must call imagination to your aid. The feeble narrow sense cannot descry innumerable worlds revolving round the central fires; and in those worlds the energy of an all-perfect mind displayed in endless forms. But neither sense nor imagination are big enough to comprehend the boundless extent with all its glittering furniture. Though the labouring mind exert and strain each power to its utmost reach, there still stands out ungrasped a surplusage immeasurable. Yet all the vast bodies that compose this mighty frame, how distant and remote soever, are by some secret mechanism, some divine art and force linked in a mutual dependence and Intercourse with each other, even with this earth, which was almost slipt from my thoughts, and lost in the crowd of worlds. Is not the whole system immense, beautiful, glorious beyond expression and beyond thought! What treatment then do those philosophers deserve, who would deprive these noble and delightful scenes of all reality? How should those principles be entertained, that lead us to think all the visible beauty of the creation a false imaginary glare? To be plain, can you expect this scepticism of yours will not be thought extravagantly absurd by all men of sense? (*D* II: 210–11)

Hylas cannot yet comprehend what Philonous is telling him in this speech: he is still caught in a self-pitying sceptical malaise. But we can. As the 'First Dialogue' made clear, our sense perceptions do not naturally signify external bodies. Instead, when we allow them to signify, and cease to impose conventional philosophical significance on them, we recognize that they are not just simple perceptions, but rather a variety of more complex but inseparable sensations and feelings ('sooths', 'delights'). This is a further consequence of Berkeley's argument that pain/pleasure and sensation cannot be abstracted from one another. Instead, pains and pleasures are particular and connected to particular sensations, which give rise to signs through emotions ('pleasing horror') and result in judgments ('agreeable wildness'). It is all so natural to us that we don't even notice how meaningful it is, and how at odds with a reductionist and materialist picture of the world.

With Philonous' speech, Berkeley is implicitly contrasting his synoptic vision of how and what the world means with a materialist mechanist such as Fontenelle. Berkeley's description of countless worlds that we begin to glimpse with a telescope, surpassing our senses, is very much in line with Fontenelle's, and certainly not dismissive of the new science. But for Berkeley, unlike for Fontenelle (for whom these signify only the many ways in which atoms can concatenate to produce more complex bodies), they are signs of a larger and greater purpose. They mean something different. A materialist of the Fontenelle type has difficulties explaining teleological purposes or the relations between parts and wholes, in that mechanism is normally construed solely in terms of blind efficient causes.

Like Shaftesbury, of whom Berkeley was highly critical, the whole and context provide more, teleological meanings:

> WHEN we reflect on any ordinary Frame or Constitution either of Art or Nature; and consider how hard it is to give the least account of a particular Part, without a competent Knowledge of the Whole: Whole and Parts. We need not wonder to find ourselves at a loss in many things relating to the Constitution and Frame of Nature herself.[85]

In this influential passage Shaftesbury is arguing that although we can have reasonably good knowledge of the internal workings of individuals, without knowledge of the whole as such we cannot understand our place in the larger workings of nature. The Lockean worry that we cannot in principle know the internal material constitutions of things or their real essence, much the less their ultimate purpose, is offset by the fact that we can know their particular structure and purpose in a limited way. And, from judging their individual structure, we can know what their virtues are, i.e., what it is to function well as that sort of thing.

Berkeley rejected Shaftesbury's identification of individual structure and virtue, and instead tried to argue for more global meanings. This is evident from Philonous' claim that 'while they mutually aid and support, do they not also set off and illustrate each other?' Relations between parts and whole are not solely relations of dependence and superiority, or functional interaction, but also the basis for broader, comparative judgments. Berkeley adds that the relation between part and whole concerns both the 'crowd of worlds' and the place of Earth within the 'crowd'. Through comparing and connecting parts and wholes we see that 'Earth' is not just a word which stands in for an idea signifying a rotating globe of adhering corpuscles, but rather signs refer to other signs and raise wonder at the standpoint of humility and awe.

Later, in *Alciphron* and the *New Theory of Vision Revisited*, Berkeley would argue that our perceptions of nature (particularly visual perceptions) *are* God speaking to us, and that nature is God's language:

> The Great Mover and Author of Nature constantly explaineth himself to the Eyes of Men, by the sensible intervention of arbitrary Signs, which have no Similitude or Connexion with the things signified; so as by compounding and disposing them, to suggest an endless variety of Objects differing in nature, time, and place, thereby informing and directing Men, how to act with respect to things distant and future, as well as near and future. (*A* IV.12)[86]

In the discussion in *Alciphron*, Alciphron asks why the signs seem both arbitrary (which is the pre-condition for Berkeley for it being a language) and at the same time regular or natural. Berkeley's mouthpiece Euphranor responds that Alciphron should look in a mirror in order to understand.[87] This language is arbitrary, in that God has organized heterogeneous signs which do not resemble one another to produce meaning (such as tactile sensations and visual experience to produce judgments of distance). But it is also natural in that it has been organized to be understood and interpreted by us in accordance with our natures.

So, as opposed to Shaftesbury, whose account tended to make God extraneous by concentrating on local function, Berkeley underscored the role of God both in global meaning and in sentiments arising from comparison. On Berkeley's account, God is quite literally the 'Author of Nature' (*D* II: 210, *P* 147), and to perceive is to read God's book. This does not mean that it is obvious to everyone that God is the author of the visual language of nature through which he communicates to creatures. Berkeley thinks this only becomes evident upon reflection.

The passages from *Alciphron* are consistent with Philonous' speech (Berkeley is a remarkably consistent philosopher over the course of his career), although Berkeley does not invoke this theory in the *Dialogues*. Philonous' speech also begins to hint towards an interesting argument from design: that nature is so wondrous, and the arbitrary language so well-organized and meaningful, that it could not have happened by accident, but must have a designer and meaning-maker. Unsurprisingly then, the discussion moves to God.

God (211–15)

A materialist picture has difficulties in proving the existence of the sort of God that an ordinary religious person might want beyond the earth and the crowd of worlds. Spinoza had a number of proofs of God in the *Ethics*,[88] but they could be taken to prove at most that an all-encompassing Nature exists, certainly not that a Christian (or Jewish or Muslim or Buddhist or Hindu) God exists. The same could also be said of Descartes' proofs of God in the *Meditations*. Descartes argued for an all-powerful first principle, but that this first principle was omniscient or Good was more questionable. Readers were also disturbed, wrongly or rightly, by the voluntarist character of Descartes' God: it seemed as if the world was only good because God made it, and consequently the anxiety that the theory sanctioned a God who need not be good by ordinary measures, and a world that was unworthy of a truly good God. Locke's argument in the *Essay* (*E* IV.10) was even more threadbare: it showed that God was omniscient, omnipotent, eternal and thinking. But although Locke concluded the proof with a number of arguments that God cannot be material, his admission that we cannot be sure, however improbable, that matter does not think (*E* IV.3.6) undermined his sincerity. The problem of how to get a good and immaterial God, not just a big Will, from a metaphysical proof is longstanding, and not just particular to Christianity. Maimonides, Crescas, Avicenna, Averroes, and many others in the Islamic philosophical tradition (which included Jewish philosophers as well) struggled with how to do this before Christian philosophers took up the questions (as did philosophers in other religious traditions).

The most famous proof of God's existence in the early eighteenth century was Samuel Clarke's *A Demonstration of the Being and Attributes of God* (1704), given as the initiating series of Boyle lectures to counteract the tide of atheism. Clarke's argument was *a priori* (i.e., unlike an argument from design it presumed nothing about the world other than the rather general claim that 'something exists from all eternity'), and very formal. In Proposition VI Clarke showed that the 'self-existent being must of necessity be infinite and omnipresent'.[89] About the time that Berkeley's *Principles* appeared, the young Joseph Butler (later Bishop Butler) wrote a series of letters to Clarke criticizing the argument, beginning by pointing out that a 'self-existent being' need not of necessity be omnipresent, since it could exist for all eternity but in different places (i.e., now here, now there, but always somewhere as opposed to here, there, and everywhere).[90] Butler would go on to rise well above Berkeley in the Anglican church hierarchy, and to write the most famous of eighteenth-century arguments from design, the *Analogy of Religion* (1736), where he claimed that the existence of a revealed God could be shown to be likely on the basis of probable evidence (as opposed to Clarke's necessary reasons). Butler's *Analogy of Religion* is an important opponent for (and sophisticated influence on) many of Hume's arguments against the probable evidence of revealed or natural religion.

Berkeley's initial proof is extremely brief: in fact, it hardly seems a proof at all. He presented a brief argument from design in *Principles* 146, but the first argument in the *Dialogues* is even simpler:

> Philonous: To me it is evident, for the reasons you allow of, that sensible things cannot exist otherwise than in a mind or spirit. Whence I conclude, not that they have no real existence, but that seeing they depend not on my thought, and have an existence distinct from being perceived by me, *there must be some other mind wherein they exist.* As sure therefore as the sensible world really exists, so sure is there an infinite omnipresent spirit who contains and supports it.
> Hylas: What! this is no more than I and all Christians hold; nay, and all others too who believe there is a God, and that he knows and comprehends all things.
> Philonous: Ay, but here lies the difference. Men commonly believe that all things are known or perceived by God, because they believe the being of a God, whereas I on the other side, immediately and necessarily conclude the being of a God, because all sensible things must be perceived by him.

Hylas has accepted, wrongly or rightly, that sensible things can only exist in a mind. He and Philonous both wish to hold that sensible things have a distinct existence as well. If: (1) they can only exist in a mind; and (2) if to exist is to have an existence distinct from each of our particular perceptions; and finally (3) if sensible things exist, then (4) '*there must be some other mind wherein they exist.*'[91]

Berkeley is trying to show that the existence of the sort of God a Christian might want follows 'with a direct and immediate demonstration, from a most evident principle', i.e., Berkeley's own account of perception. But even if we do hold that (1) has been established, and that (2) is desirable, and we even hold that (3) is unquestionable, (4) is still suspect as a conclusion. First, Butler's objection to Clarke could be modified against Berkeley. Why couldn't it be the case that different perceivers all perceive objects at different times, preserving the continuity of objects without recourse to one omnipresent omniperceiver? Indeed, Berkeley's ideas about the relational character of space might point in this direction by analogy. Just as we can describe space through the relation of multiple bodies without reference to one fixed reference point, so perceptions of bodies might arise from multiple perceivers without recourse to one encompassing spectator. There would be minds and objects of those minds, but not an über-mind. Many more objections could be offered. Isn't Berkeley trying to avoid the consequence that when a tree falls in the forest and no one perceives it, it does not exist? But why shouldn't he just accept this? Indeed, in framing this proof aren't we violating the constraints of the 'Master Argument'? Aren't we trying to account for things we do not perceive with an omnipresent omniperceiver? But then aren't we trying to perceive something we do not perceive – trees beyond our perception necessitating the omnipresent omniperceiver?

Berkeley will respond to the objection that he should just embrace solipsism by arguing that two features of ideas point towards some perceiver beyond me. First, I often experience them independent of my will – I acquire them adventitiously. This was an important criterion of externality for both Descartes and Locke (*E* IV.9.3), that I acquire the ideas in a manner beyond my control and therefore they could not be produced by me. Second, if I did produce the ideas they would have to arise from the imagination. But when I imagine things, the experience is far less vivid than, and parasitic on, my experiences through the senses. The second argument is questionable on Cartesian grounds: if we have experienced extremely vivid dreams and hallucinations, how can we be so sure that the products of the imagination are less vivid than waking experiences? Hume would later take up the distinction between degrees of vivacity of our ideas from Berkeley, but use it to argue for a thoroughgoing scepticism: the difference between reality and illusion is just a matter of a degree of psychological force. Similar arguments can be used against the first point as well. Does the fact that I don't want something, and experience it independent of my will, really mean that it's not produced by me? If that's the case I would never have a headache!

Philonous supplements the proof with a further argument:

An infinite mind should be necessarily inferred from the bare existence of the sensible world . . . to them only who have made this easy reflexion: That the sensible world is that which we perceive by our several senses; and that nothing is perceived by the senses beside ideas; and that no idea or archetype of an idea can exist otherwise than in a mind. (*D* II: 212)

Here the steps are: (1) we perceive the sensible world with several senses; (2) nothing is perceived by the senses except ideas; from which follows (3) no archetype of an idea exists without a mind. There is a missing step presumed (2A), that an *archetype* of an idea is sufficiently idea-like that it too must be perceived by a mind.

As we discussed briefly when considering Malebranche as one of Berkeley's influences, there is a long tradition of presuming that things must have archetypes in order for God to choose to create them. Malebranche suggests that God gives us access to these archetypes in order to understand the material world. But Berkeley cannot draw on this tradition as the basis for an argument for the existence of God since, as the example of Malebranche makes clear, the tradition presumes the existence of God. We might think that archetype here means not a divine archetype, but whatever provides an independent unity of our varied perceptions through different heterogeneous senses in such a manner that we experience them as unities, re-identify them, etc., and that he wants this concept to do some technical work. But I don't think this is right either.

Instead, Berkeley seems to be saying that if you use a concept like archetype, whether a Malebranchian objective idea in the mind of God or an archetype or pattern of a thing in the external world, then this archetype presumes a mind. As was the case with the arguments against abstract ideas, Berkeley's strategy is to ferret out modern assumptions and to show that the moderns share immaterialist commitments, whether they like it or not. In this case whatever archetype theory you hold, the archetype doesn't get you beyond needing a perceiver God.

This was also a challenge to philosophers whom Berkeley considered atheists: Spinoza, Hobbes, and Lucilio Vanini (the Renaissance anti-scholastic who was burned at the stake in 1619). If they 'conceive how so much as a rock, a desert, a chaos, or confused jumble of atoms; how any thing at all, either sensible or imaginable, can exist independent of a mind' (*D* II: 213), they should also see that their atheism is flawed. Berkeley seems to be suggesting that, like it or not, their theories depend on perceivers, and if they have any stable, persistent and basic category in their theories, which they use to build up the others (such as atoms) it must be perceived in a unified way: and this presumes God. Certainly, none of Berkeley's atheists would be likely to accept Berkeley's arguments. Berkeley seems more to be suggesting to followers of Locke and Malebranche and other more moderate moderns that these theories are dreadfully flawed and that Berkeley's own philosophy makes the flaws even more readily apparent than the modern systems.

More generally, we should understand Berkeley's arguments for God as trying to show the proximity of God to us, as opposed to philosophers he understood to be deists (like Collins and Shaftesbury) who wrote God out of the world, while at the same time avoiding lapsing into Malebranche's position that we actually see God's ideas. The Divine Language theory does just this, in that our visual language is made by God to communicate to us, but it is not God.

Malebranche: passive ideas, vision in God, and occasionalism (214–16)

In order to underscore the difference, Berkeley has Hylas agree that Philonous' argument is 'highly serviceable to religion', but also has him note that Berkeley's arguments appear very similar to Malebranche's 'seeing all things in God'. Berkeley's early reviewers noted this as well. The late seventeenth and early eighteenth century was a time of great popularity for Malebranche's philosophy. Locke wrote a critical commentary on Malebranche's account of seeing all things in God in 1690, and the British Malebranchian John Norris had published the second volume of his *An essay towards the theory of the ideal or intelligible world* (1701–4) less than ten years before the publication of the *Dialogues*.

Berkeley had tried to distinguish his doctrine from Malebranche's in the *Principles* (*P* 148), but apparently to little success. Ironically, in the *Dialogues* Berkeley makes Philonous unfamiliar with the Malebranchian doctrine, and has Hylas explain it to him. On Hylas' account Malebranche holds that since we are spiritual beings and incapable of union with matter, God gives us access to the archetypal perfections on the basis of which material objects have been created. These perfections are purely spiritual, immaterial and so capable of immediate union with our souls. We perceive them better or worse due to our own minds and perceptual abilities, but God gives us access to them through his grace. Through them we have knowledge of the otherwise inaccessible material world.

Philonous immediately responds to Hylas that since ideas are 'passive and inert', they cannot be in God who is purely active. Berkeley discussed the passive character of our ideas in the *Principles*:

> All our ideas, sensations, notions, or the things which we perceive . . . are visibly inactive – there is nothing of power or agency included in them. So that one idea or object of thought cannot produce or make any alteration in another. To be satisfied of the truth of this, there is nothing else requisite but a bare observation of our ideas. For, since they and every part of them exist only in the mind, it follows that there is nothing in them but what is perceived: but whoever shall attend to his ideas, whether of sense or reflexion, will not perceive in them any power or activity; there is, therefore, no such thing contained in them. (*P* 26)

Since ideas are *just* what a perceiver perceives them to be (a questionable corollary of Berkeley's claim that all that we perceive are ideas), to be an idea is *just* to be perceived by a perceiver. It is a questionable corollary because from 'all we perceive are ideas' it does not follow that ideas are *just* what a perceiver perceives them to be, or that to be an idea is just to be perceived – or, indeed, that they are passive. Berkeley thought that he had arguments for claiming that ideas are just what a perceiver perceives them to be: 'since they and every part of them exist only in the mind, it follows that there is nothing in them but what is perceived.' The intermediate step is then that 'ideas exist only in the mind', a thesis he has argued for over the course of the 'First Dialogue'. Berkeley's brief argument suggests that he thought that 'to be an idea is just to be perceived by a perceiver' drops out nearly tautologously from 'ideas exist only in the mind'.

Let's assume that Berkeley has established that 'ideas exist only in the mind'. Does it really follow that to be an idea is just to be perceived by a perceiver? Or that they are passive? As to the latter, he may have in mind Malebranche's famous argument for occasionalism in 'Elucidation XV': that there is nothing in bodies taken singly on the basis of which we can attribute powers to them. If we inspect two billiard balls we will never find the force that can pass from one to the other in their qualities. This argument holds by extension of sensible ideas, since they are the qualities of bodies in which we are searching for power or force, and nothing besides these qualities. Or he may be drawing on the general shared early modern presupposition (which we have discussed before) that sense perceptions are inert. But it is by no means evident that by simply attending to our ideas we will see that there is no notion of power and activity in them. Berkeley's thought seems to be that they just are our perceptions of them, and consequently there's nothing beyond our perception which could be a power. But this presumes that power or activity is nothing we perceive directly.

As to the former, we speak all the time of hidden motives unknown to the agent, and we often presume that our own minds are very opaque to us. Aren't these examples of unperceived perceptions in the sense that Hume discussed ('perceptions which are not perceived') as opposed to the sense putatively ruled out by the Master Argument ('perceiving something unperceived')?

This objection seems not to have occurred to Berkeley because, like Descartes, Locke, Malebranche, and many other early modern philosophers, he equated 'thinking' with a unified power of consciously attending to sensible qualities, facts, meanings, etc., and so would have considered the objection incoherent. This does not mean that Berkeley did not recognize that we often think in a ramshackle and confused way. For many early modern authors, passions, emotions, and sentiments were invoked to explain how thinking could become murky (and for Malebranche, how it could become elevated as well). But that's different from suggesting that we are unconsciously thinking of something while we are consciously thinking about something else. The very term 'unconscious' entered collo-quial use with Freud, and although some have argued that there are glimmerings of a similar notion in Hume, Leibniz, and Spinoza, these glimmerings – such as they are – were very far from ordinary.

One tacit reason for the general agreement among modern philo-sophers that thinking was a unified conscious power has to do with moral responsibility. If it is the case that I can have motives that are not conscious, or I can be thinking about something and not recog-nize it, it becomes very hard to impute moral responsibility to me. And, if there is no unity to my thinking it is hard to judge me as a unified subject of moral appraisal. There is of course the interesting issue of original sin, which many Christian philosophers struggled to explain in terms of corruption or failure of conscious processes (as opposed to unconscious impediments). Notably, of the three philo-sophers who are associated with (perhaps) having a doctrine of uncon-scious motivation, two of them (Hume and Spinoza) rejected this kind of picture of morality as depending on conscious grounds for moral responsibility. They also rejected the idea of a unified soul, eternal and separable from the body, which was also connected with this picture.

There is also a connection between conceiving the mind as unified and fully conscious and anti-innatism of the sort that holds that we cannot have deep thoughts in our minds which we then draw out. If this was the case then we would have thoughts which were in our minds and yet which we did not perceive or think until they were drawn out, even though they were in our minds all along. Some of the strongest defenders of innatism (such as Descartes) also held that the mind was a unified, conscious power, in part in connection with arguments for the separability of the soul. But Cartesians like Malebranche found the position incoherent, and rejected innatism. Surprisingly then, Berkeley was fairly agnostic on the question of innate ideas – particularly surprising given that he is rarely agnostic! As we've noted previously, he thought that Locke's beginning the *Essay* with a criticism of innate ideas had bad consequences for the rest of the work. There are passages in *Siris* where he seems to accept a Platonic doctrine of innate ideas, and portrays them in rather baroque terms. But upon closer inspection he only explicitly accepted what fit in with his own account of perception:

And as the Platonic philosophy supposed intellectual notions to be originally inexistent or innate in the soul, so likewise it supposed sensible qualities to exist (though not originally) in the soul, and there only. (*S* 316)

Berkeley went on to distinguish ancient theories of innate ideas from the sort of account of innate ideas that modern philosophers (presumably Locke and Malebranche) rejected. His point seemed to be that in rejecting innate ideas, philosophers drew the unwarranted inference that ideas must come from the 'outside', which is false as well (and indeed potentially incoherent without a further explanation of what outside means).

Berkeley may not have wished to rule out innate ideas in the sense of propensities or dispositions for reasons to do with his divine language theory. Indeed, he concludes this section of the discussion by stating his proof succinctly in a different form, linking the *a priori* argument for a divine unifying perceiver to an *a posteriori* argument from the providential and governed design of the world:

> *There is a mind which affects me every moment with all the sensible impressions I perceive.* And from the variety, order, and manner of these, I conclude the author of them to be *wise, powerful, and good beyond comprehension.* Mark it well; I do not say, I see things by perceiving that which represents them in the intelligible substance of God. This I do not understand; but I say, The things by me perceived are known by the understanding, and produced by the will, of an infinite spirit. (*D* II: 215)

In other words, the perceptions I have, which have been produced by the Divine Spirit and placed into me, exhibit an order which shows that their author is the sort of God we might want, as opposed to a malicious demon. They exhibit not just power but wisdom (the divine understanding) and goodness (the divine will). I am predisposed to read these perceptions in this cogent manner and they make the world meaningful.

Berkeley presumes here that he has shown that these perceptions are exhibited to me by God. They must exist in some mind, we do not produce them, and so they must be produced by another mind. But it is not at all clear what it means for an idea to be produced by a mind and then exhibited to us. Again the analogy with language seems to be doing some work. God perceives them and then communicates whatever is relevant to us for us to perceive. But even if we accept all of Berkeley's arguments, does this clearly follow? And what does it really mean for an idea to be actively made to be passive?

In sum there are reasons why for Berkeley the perceiver, not the idea, is the active power, as opposed to Malebranche, for whom the idea itself is active, even if the arguments are questionable. For Malebranche this is a metaphysical solution to a Cartesian problem: how to deal with our access to the external world if there is no interaction between mind and matter, and how to hold that truths are objective as such, not just for this or that mind. Berkeley's rejection is based not on metaphysical objections (even if metaphysical issues are in the background) but on arguments from the nature of perception. Despite their similarities, which were greater than Berkeley might have liked, they have very different affinities.

This was only Berkeley's first objection! Philonous also offered an internal criticism of Malebranche's theory: that if God grants us access to His ideas, which are the archetypes of material objects, this makes material objects extraneous. Malebranche argued that God's creation was ordered to maximize simplicity and efficiency, on the basis of which he explained the simplicity of laws of rectilinear motion and other phenomena.[92] But if this is the case, then according to Berkeley God has not acted in the simplest manner, since the existence of matter is to no purpose and all could be more efficiently explained just by ideas.

The brief discussion of Malebranche's philosophy concludes with Philonous' admission that he is not 'surprised, if some Men imagine that I run into the enthusiasm of Malbranche, though in truth I am very remote from it' (*D* II: 214). The philosophers differed on abstract ideas, the external world and the testimony of our senses, although notably Berkeley differed with Locke on these questions as well – so it does not say as much about his specific divergences from Berkeley as Berkeley might have liked.

Know not what, know not why (217–26)

The remainder of the 'Second Dialogue' is primarily concerned with refuting positions that argue for matter as an occasional or intermediate cause of ideas. More accurately, it is Berkeley's attempt to demonstrate that philosophical positions that might seem to be consistent with his own in fact use 'matter' in questionable ways, and to show the reader how to reason properly about them. As we just saw,

Berkeley thinks it is very important that God is immediately in our world, although we are not in God. Each layer of matter smuggled in by philosophers adds additional weight to the curtain of words.

Hylas begins by suggesting that there might be a third entity besides active spirits and passive ideas – matter – and that matter has a limited role as cause, instrument (general or particular), or occasion of ideas. By using 'instrument', Berkley perhaps means to invoke Newton and Clarke, and the theory that space is a divine instrument or *sensorium*, subordinate to spirit but the means by which God knows and acts omnipresently. Berkeley sent a copy of the *Principles* to Clarke, who never responded as far as we know. By 'occasion' Berkeley means to invoke Malebranche's occasionalism, but also Cartesianism more generally. Philonous objects that all of these uses of 'matter' alter the accepted usage, and that by altering the use Hylas is just falling back on his old, bad philosophical habits. Philonous accordingly argues against these objections in the same way he has against other objections: that ultimately all of these intermediate entities rest on, or are, sensible qualities, and that God can act without needing intermediaries.

In this context Berkeley introduces a version of the principle of sufficient reason: 'It is to me a sufficient Reason not to believe the Existence of any thing, if I see no Reason for believing it.' Philonous goes on further to remark that neither a philosopher nor a 'Man of common sense' should 'pretend to believe you know not what, and you know not why'. The principle of sufficient reason was associated with Cartesians, and particularly with Spinoza and Leibniz. Berkeley's version is a negative, epistemic principle of sufficient reason: that I am warranted in *believing* that some thing does *not* exist if I see no reason for believing that the thing exists. Berkeley seems to presume the positive version as well: that I am warranted in believing that some thing exists if there is a reason for it to exist. Philonous applies the principle to matter: if there is no good reason to hold that matter exists, then that is a sufficient reason to conclude matter does not exist. If all of Hylas' objections can be shown to be without warrant, then that alone will be a good reason to deny that matter exists.

The crucial difference from Leibniz and Spinoza is that Berkeley presents not a metaphysical principle but an epistemic one, in that it concerns well-founded and ill-founded beliefs and the arguments that follow from them. An epistemic principle about the warrant of belief should not slide into a metaphysical principle about what necessarily is without further justification. Berkeley is usually careful to allow the principle to slide.

All beliefs in matter are by this token poorly founded, in that they are cases where we 'know not what' matter is, and 'know not why' it is used. The epistemic principle of sufficient reason seems much too strong though, since it seems to rule out God causing our particular sense ideas. Why would God need to create a web of passive sense perceptions when He could communicate with His creatures even more directly? Of course Berkeley could respond that we *do* perceive passive ideas, and given that we do this is the best explanation, and at the very least far better than these competing explanations. But why not take the next step towards a 'direct realist' theory, get rid of passive ideas entirely, and suppose that we perceive neither ideas, nor matter, but tables, chairs, trees, and chipmunks?[93] Furthermore, it always seems that there might be a better explanation.

Berkeley presents a number of arguments that draw on the principle of sufficient reason. They take the form: Do you really know what the thing you are discussing is, and can you offer a reason why it should exist? For example:

> I desire that, beside what has been hitherto suggested, you will farther consider whether, upon supposition that matter exists, you can possibly conceive how you should be affected by it? Or supposing it did not exist, whether it be not evident you might for all that be affected with the same ideas you now are, and consequently have the very same reasons to believe its existence that you now can have? (*D* II: 221)

In other words: Do you really know what it means to be affected by matter, and can you offer a reason why it should exist given that it would seem to change nothing at all? If you can't, then your belief is unwarranted. Through reading the 'Second Dialogue' we take part in Hylas' education in what qualifies as a reason, in how to reason consistently, and in the necessity of reasons guiding beliefs. The words 'reason' and 'reasoning' occur over and over again in the 'Second Dialogue', and at one point when Hylas admits that even though he knows that matter does not exist, he cannot help but believe that it does exist, Philonous notes that 'there is need of time and pains: The attention must be awakened and detained by a frequent repetition of the same thing placed oft in the same, oft in different lights.' This is because reasons are offered as counterballast to stubborn beliefs: the stubborn beliefs arise from a 'Stain of Prejudice' and sloppy changes in the meanings of words feed the prejudice and allow the ill-founded beliefs to persist – even when it is evident upon careful insection that there is no substantial support for them. As we read we are being trained to take care with meanings and to reason in the same fashion as Philonous.

The training results in Hylas moving from the characteristic statement and assent mode of the 'First Dialogue' to more active argument, most effectively against himself. For example, he responds to one of Philonous' objections thus:

> Oh Philonous! now you think you have entangled me; for if I say it exists in place, then you will infer that it exists in the mind, since it is agreed, that place or extension exists only in the mind. (*D* II: 222)

Berkeley is showing us that Hylas is learning how to reason as he begins to question the existence of matter; and conversely, that to hold that matter exists is to reason poorly and use the word 'matter' equivocally. If philosophers actually reasoned about matter in the ways that they proscribed that we ought to reason about all subjects, they would realize that they know little or nothing about it ('it lies beneath', 'it supports'), have no reason for positing it when ideas will do the job as well, and ought to banish it. Matter in fact has been a constraint on reasoning.

Towards the end of the 'Second Dialogue', Philonous enumerates the ways in which Hylas has tried to preserve a role for matter in his theory:

> Pray tell me if the case stands not thus: At first, from a belief of material substance you would have it that the immediate objects existed without the mind; then that they are archetypes; then causes; next instruments; then occasions: Lastly, something in general, which being interpreted proves nothing. So matter comes to nothing. (*D* II: 222–3)

The list is presented as sufficiently exhaustive that the objections of materialists should be subsumed under one or another of these categories, for each of which we can show there is neither an idea of nor a reason why. The final entry on the list is the 'general abstract idea of entity' which represents Hylas' final attempt to preserve a place for matter and a sense that there is some reality beyond ideas which anchors them, to which they refer and which they represent. Philonous asks Hylas to try to 'frame a distinct idea of entity in general, prescinded from . . . all particular things whatsoever' and Hylas fails to do so.

Berkeley wishes us to draw the conclusion that we cannot frame any of these ideas of matter, because at bottom they depend upon framing an abstract idea in order to signify something – entity as distinguished from any entity. And Berkeley thinks, rightly or wrongly, that our failure to frame such an idea means that we have a word 'entity' but no idea that the word stands in for. Philonous has been teaching us to recognize and criticize abstract ideas from his discussion of the inability to separate pain and pleasure from vehement sensations onward. In fact, the abstract idea of entity is the sort of abstract idea that even Locke viewed as meaningless when he counselled that we ought to avoid sailing into the vast ocean of being and think about our duty!

Even if the idea of entity is particularly vacuous, Berkeley suggests that none of the other apparently more credible ideas really fare much better under scrutiny:

> That from a cause, effect, operation, sign, or other circumstance, there may reasonably be inferred the existence of a thing not immediately perceived, and that it were absurd for any man to argue against the existence of that thing, from his having no direct and positive notion of it, I freely own. But where there is nothing of all this; where neither reason nor revelation induces us to believe the existence of a thing; where we have not even a relative notion of it; where an abstraction is made from perceiving and being perceived, from spirit and idea: Lastly, where there is not so much as the most inadequate or faint idea pretended to: I will not indeed thence conclude against the reality of any notion or existence of any thing: But my inference shall be, that you mean nothing at all: that you employ words to no manner of purpose, without any design or signification whatsoever. (*D* II: 223)

This is an important passage, because it makes clear that Berkeley thinks that knowledge does not depend on direct or immediate perception. In addition to positive notions, we can also have relative, notions which give us reason to think that their *relata* exists. 'Relative notion' is one of the more mysterious concepts in Berkeley's philosophy. 'Notions' simpliciter are relatively less mysterious – they sometimes refer broadly to any mental activity, but they usually refer more specifically to active thinking and reflection on the self, God and other minds as opposed to passive reception of sense perceptions. They are not ideas in Berkeley's narrow sense in that they are not images. Berkeley hardly says anything about 'relative notions' and he may just have thought that they were notions arising in us which were signified by our perceptions, through causation and other relations.[94] Many have pointed to the problem of getting relations from Berkeley's theory of mind, which only seems to have a place for particular sense perceptions and notions.

Equally importantly, Berkeley notes that lack of a reason does not mean that something necessarily does not exist – it may or it may not. This is a worry we have had about Berkeley's arguments throughout: he moves from the fact that there is no support presently available for a thing to that the thing doesn't exist. We saw this problem in the Master Argument. When we inspect a belief that someone avows and find that there are no good reasons that support it, and also find that the person who espouses the belief cannot give a clear positive or relative notion, although we cannot draw an ultimate conclusion about the existence or non-existence of some thing we can come to a *psychological* conclusion: that the words which the person is uttering signifies no ideas or things to them, and so that they are speaking nonsense.

Unfortunately, Berkeley does seem to go on to say that one can show that it is impossible that some thing exists when the concept of the thing signifies nothing:

Philonous: When is a thing shewn to be impossible?

Hylas: When a repugnancy is demonstrated between the ideas comprehended in its definition.

Philonous: But where there are no ideas, there no repugnancy can be demonstrated between ideas.

Hylas: I agree with you.

Philonous: Now in that which you call the obscure indefinite sense of the word *matter*, it is plain, by your own confession, there was included no idea at all, no sense except an unknown sense, which is the same as none. You are not therefore to expect I should prove a repugnancy between ideas where there are no ideas; or the impossibility of matter taken in an *unknown* sense, that is no sense at all. My business was only to shew, you meant *nothing*; and this you were brought to own. So that in all your various senses, you have been shewed either to mean nothing at all, or if any thing, an absurdity. And if this be not sufficient to prove the impossibility of a thing, I desire you will let me know what is. (*D* II: 225–6)

Furthermore, we can make sense of this passage if we recognize that Philonous is responding to the problem of how to prove that matter is impossible if the materialist opponent engages in a 'shifting unfair method', and so each time a particular sense of matter is shown to be impossible quickly shifts to another sense. All that one can do in these circumstances is show that each particular sense in which the opponent uses matter is impossible. For example, the belief in entity is ill founded because it is an abstract idea, and like other abstract ideas can mean nothing at all because it refers to purportedly separate concepts (that which underlies the thing, which hold of qualities, which causes, which occasion or that which just *is*) which in fact *cannot* be separated from particular sense experiences. The belief in matter as a divine instrument or *sensorium* is an absurdity, because it suggests that God would need an intermediate cause for action, which would conflict with his attributes. And so forth.

But, one cannot show a repugnance between different vacuous, absurd or inconceivable concepts because there's nothing to educe the absurdities between! At best, one can show each in turn is vacuous, absurd or inconceivable. The opponent can always shift around and refuse to commit to one meaning: in fact this is a traditional sceptical strategy. But if they are at all serious or earnest they will come to see that matter is 'impossible' in a sense set out by the initial discussions of scepticism, and that the doctrine of matter leads to more paradoxes and repugnances than immaterialism – within each of the particular definitions of matter. Given a competing doctrine that does not lead to these repugnances, and given that they mean nothing, it is impossible to coherently maintain the existence of matter, in that it is inconceivable. And when arguing with philosophers, that's likely to be the best one is going to get.

The fear is that by unmooring a stubborn belief such as the belief in the existence of matter, all the rest will tumble down and the immaterialist philosopher will become a wild-eyed, enthusiastic sceptic. Hylas expresses this fear as he leaves to think over the day's discussions. The two agree to meet the next morning.

Questions

1. Is the fact that we know not why and not what really sufficient grounds for rejection? Would it be more sensible to deny Berkeley's version of the Principle of Sufficient Reason?

2. Can you formulate a way out of Berkeley's argument that the brain cannot cause sensation? How would Berkeley respond?

3. If you find Berkeley's vision of a meaningful nature compelling, does this mean you ought to believe in God (or alternately, if you believe, does it necessarily reinforce your belief)?

THE 'THIRD DIALOGUE'

The 'Third Dialogue' is mostly more intriguing than satisfying. Fortunately it is very intriguing! Berkeley hints at theories of archetypes, of ectypes, of spirit, and notions, and an account of action, but does not really develop any of them at length. The longest sustained discussion is an account of the Mosaic creation responding to Lady Percival's query. The 'Third Dialogue' is long, so I will not attempt an exhaustive treatment. Instead I will discuss serially what Berkeley wrote on a few pivotal topics.

Hylas the sceptic (227–30)

When Philonous encounters Hylas in the garden the following day, Hylas' temper has changed. He has become a sceptic. His usually polite questions and answers have surrendered to a harder tone. What is the substance of his scepticism? Hylas claims that the search for the real essences of things is vain – 'there is not a single thing in the world, whereof we can know the real nature or what it is in itself' – and that men were not intended for speculation. He challenges all of Philonous' claims in an aggressive, sceptical fashion.

Berkeley wished us to see that the reason why Hylas has become a sceptic is that he is still holding on to the belief in matter, and on to the identification of 'real things' with 'corporeal substances'. Apparently the repetition has not done its work, and each evening Hylas has slipped back into his previous materialist beliefs. This is perhaps Berkeley's central negative philosophical lesson, that the modern philosophy entails scepticism and needs strong argumentative medicine! Berkeley thought that Locke had posited a causually, ontologically and constitutively prior world of matter and corpuscles that we cannot ever know in itself, nor fully access. Malebranche argued that although our knowledge of the material world is merely probable, and we can never access it directly, it is undeniable and our experience of even divine ideas and divine occasions are in its service. For Berkeley these philosophers, and others, attempt to explain what they do know on the basis of what they admittedly cannot. And scepticism is the unsurprising result.

Philonous teases: 'surely, Hylas, I can distinguish gold, for example, from iron?' (*D* II: 227). This was the example that Locke used in his discussion of the difference between nominal and real essences, the discussion that is tacitly being invoked by Hylas to support his scepticism. A difference that is knowable by an empirical test, such as dissolving gold in *aqua regia,* only involves 'nominal essences' or the ways in which we organize the qualities we perceive for our use and benefit, and does not involve the deep structure or real essences of individuals or classes, which is wholly inaccessible to us. In *Essay* III.6, Locke argued that sortal terms, the words we use to sort the world into classes and kinds, and species are always set by nominal essences and appearances:

> It is true, I have often mentioned a real essence, distinct in substances from those abstract ideas of them, which I call their nominal essence. By this real essence I mean, that real constitution of anything, which is the foundation of all those properties that are combined in, and are constantly found to co-exist with the nominal essence; that particular constitution which everything has within itself, without any relation to anything without it. But essence, even in this sense, relates to a sort, and supposes a species. For, being that real constitution on which the properties depend, it necessarily supposes a sort of things, properties belonging only to species, and not to individuals: e.g. supposing the nominal essence of gold to be a body of such a peculiar colour and weight, with malleability and fusibility, the real essence is that constitution of the parts of matter on which these qualities and their union depend; and is also the foundation of its solubility in aqua regia and other properties, accompanying that complex

idea. Here are essences and properties, but all upon supposition of a sort or general abstract idea, which is considered as immutable; but there is no individual parcel of matter to which any of these qualities are so annexed as to be essential to it or inseparable from it. That which is essential belongs to it as a condition whereby it is of this or that sort: but take away the consideration of its being ranked under the name of some abstract idea, and then there is nothing necessary to it, nothing inseparable from it. Indeed, as to the real essences of substances, we only suppose their being, without precisely knowing what they are; but that which annexes them still to the species is the nominal essence, of which they are the supposed foundation and cause. (*E* III.VI.6)

In this passage, one can see the heart of why Berkeley had such distaste for abstract ideas, and why he thought that Locke's *Essay* would have looked different had Locke begun by considering language and essence. Here in Book III of the *Essay*, Locke is beginning to harvest the sceptical fruits of his earlier misguided labours, all the more so in Book IV. Abstract general ideas are nothing real or in the world but conventions used to sort things. We often use general words since they conduce to our utility and benefit, but that does not mean that they stand in for any one idea, much less for things or substantial beings. In fact we do not know what real essences are, except as foundation and cause of nominal essences. Berkeley concluded that there aren't any material, real essences beyond our perceptions, or any unperceived archetypes. Locke himself thought that there were cases where nominal and real essences were identical. Both moral ideas and mathematical ideas were examples of what Locke referred to as 'mixed modes'. In each of these cases, the real essence was identical with the nominal essence, albeit for different reasons.

Berkeley's diagnosis of passages like this is that the desire for a real essence, independent of nominal essences, follows from a belief in corporeal substances that we do not have access to. This splits the world into two: real and nominal essence, body and representative idea, archetype or ectype (i.e., model and sensibly perceived manifestation). And this further bred the anxiety in Descartes' *Sixth Meditation* that the people we see in the street are in fact machines, or in Malebranche's acceptance of the only probable existence of a material world. Immaterialism, on the other hand, presupposes nothing beyond thoughts: either immediate perceptions, or positive and relative notions. If a sceptic responds that this leaves the immaterialist just with ideas (taken broadly and non-technically to include notions) – *sole ideas* – the immaterialist can respond in turn that ideas are 'just' only when they are viewed in opposition to a material world that is somehow more *real*. The sceptical problem arises from a misconceived opposition, and the problem is dissolved when the opposition is recognized. This dialectical therapy results in the ability to see what the sensible world actually means.

Snow is white and man is created (227–30, 250–6)

Berkeley goes on to suggest that his philosophy is far better equipped to deal with claims like 'snow is white', 'fire is hot', and the 'real things are those very things I see and feel'. He means by this that snow just is our perception of white among other perceptions, and fire just is our perception of hot among other perceptions. Fire and snow are amalgams of particular sensible perceptions, and nothing beyond them. As intriguing as this suggestion is, there are (at least) two serious problems. First, if ideas of perceived things, such as snow and fire, are ultimately the particular sensible perceptions that make them up (since their unity cannot arise from an underlying substance), and if these perceptions are continually shifting and changing (as we saw in the 'First Dialogue'), then how can we possibly hold that 'snow is white'? Wouldn't this undermine the previous arguments?

The second objection is potentially more damaging. What gives unity to 'white snow' such that I can claim not just 'I am now experiencing a particular shade which I call white, some feelings of particular cold and solid but crunchy' and so on, but rather claim: 'Snow is white over time, re-identifiable as white snow, and snow is white even when I am not looking'? This is a further worry behind Hume's 'Scepticism of the senses', where he attempted to explain the unity of the individual over time (and the feeling I have that they persist when I am not looking at them) with associative psychology, and thus to avoid any claim to there being snow out there, somewhere, ever white. But Berkeley does not forego this claim.

Margaret Atherton has what I think is an excellent response to the first objection. Instead of thinking that 'snow is white' means that there is one colour 'white', which is always and ever predicated of snow, instead take 'white' as a cluster of shades and colours that relate to one another, 'and each of which can be reliably anticipated in appropriate circumstances'.[95] The same could be said of other qualities ascribed to snow and perceived through and by different senses. The interconnection of different particular experiences both allows us to claim 'this is snow' and gives us reason to believe 'this is white'. We could also explain 'fire is hot' in a similar manner.

This seems a plausible, and Berkeleyin solution. The problem still remains of deciding on what basis we then can judge that all of these shades resemble each other in being 'white': but this is not a problem particular to Berkeley. One solution I've already mentioned is Hume's pairwise comparisons of particular colours. Atherton goes on to note that if we adopt her account of 'snow is white', then Berkeley's discussion of microscopy later in the 'Third Dialogue' can be reconciled with his earlier claims about microscopy in the 'First Dialogue'. In the 'First Dialogue', Berkeley used arguments drawing on how different the colours of objects are when they are placed under a microscope, and the aforementioned thought experiment of looking at an object with one eye through a microscope and the other unaided, to show that colours are mind dependent. As we saw, Philonous praises telescopes in his lengthy speech in the 'Second Dialogue', and shows how through them we perceive a wide variety of things that give rise to moral and religious emotions, which in turn connect with other perceptions to signify grander and more important feelings. Berkeley's point is that we have to be attentive to what is actually being signified.

In the 'Third Dialogue' Berkeley takes up the example of the microscope again:

Strictly speaking, Hylas, we do not see the same object that we feel; neither is the same object perceived by the microscope, which was by the naked eye. But in case every variation was thought sufficient to constitute a new kind or individual, the endless number or confusion of names would render language impracticable. Therefore to avoid this as well as other inconveniences which are obvious upon a little thought, men combine together several ideas, apprehended by divers senses, or by the same sense at different times, or in different circumstances, but observed however to have some connexion in nature, either with respect to coexistence or succession; all which they refer to one name, and consider as one thing. Hence it follows that when I examine by my other senses a thing I have seen, it is not in order to understand better the same object which I had perceived by sight, the object of one sense not being perceived by the other senses. And when I look through a microscope, it is not that I may perceive more clearly what I perceived already with my bare eyes, the object perceived by the glass being quite different from the former. But in both cases my aim is only to know what ideas are connected together; and the more a man knows of the connexion of ideas, the more he is said to know of the nature of things. What therefore if our ideas are variable; what if our senses are not in all circumstances affected with the same appearances? It will not thence follow, they are not to be trusted, or that they are inconsistent either with themselves or any thing else, except it be with your preconceived notion of (I know not what) one single, unchanged, inperceivable, real nature, marked by each name. (*D* 245)

This passage affirms one of the main doctrines of the *New Theory of Vision*, that the object we see under a microscope is indeed a different object from what we see with our unassisted eyes. And just as Berkeley claimed before for the telescope, here he notices that the microscope discovers causes and connections among things that tell us about the nature of things. In contradistinction to the moderns' belief that a microscope might inform us about deep structure and real essences, Berkeley has the microscope show us larger and larger clusters of ideas, which give rise to feelings and make for meaning. We can really trust our senses if we know what to ask them: 'Will this burn me?', 'Is this sublime?', and so on.[96] If we ask a microscope for ultimate structure we will just be led to paradox and scepticism – that a feather or a hair which appears to have a colour at the micro-level has different colours or is transparent at the micro-level.

Near the end of the 'Third Dialogue', Berkeley adds:

Upon this supposition indeed, the objections from the change of colours in a pigeon's neck, or the appearance of the broken oar in the water, must be allowed to have weight. But those and the like objections vanish, if we do not maintain the being of absolute external originals, but place the reality of things in ideas, fleeting indeed, and changeable; however not changed at random, but according to the fixed order of nature. For herein consists that constancy and truth of things, which secures all the concerns of life, and distinguishes that which is real from the irregular visions of the fancy. (*D* II: 258)

The objections from the pigeon's neck and the bent oar were standard ancient sceptical objections.[97] Berkeley is arguing that sceptical consequences only arise when we seek absolute stable colours or absolute stable things, as opposed to a fixed or regular sequence of changes. This points towards the real, (broadly) moral and instrumental purpose of sense perceptions from where they gain their unity – 'to secure all the concerns of life'.

But the holism of Berkeley's solution magnifies the second objection. If all of our ideas are variable, and if they make meanings and signify emotions through the ways in which they connect with and refer to other ideas, it should then be incumbent on Berkeley to provide a theory of relations, which he does not, beyond asserting that they are relative notions. And, relations between what? If everything is variable and shifting, if each sense has its own object and each magnification or perhaps even each glimpse has its own object (for what is to distinguish looking through a telescope from any other look?), then what is being related? This is reminiscent of Berkeley's own argument for the impossibility of materialism: if each concept being related is really nothing, no contradiction will ensue, but nothing will be said at all. Chunks or islands of meaning just seem to emerge.

The stopping points on perception are the *minima* particular to each sense, although the *minima* go unmentioned in the *Three Dialogues*. Of course, one could reasonably ask what sets the *minima* and how we can talk about the identity of *minima* across different perceivers. It has a bit of the feel of taking objective, perceptual atoms for granted in a heavily perspectival theory. But still, the fact that Berkeley holds there are *minima* and that they are just the discriminatory thresholds of our senses is reasonable enough. The problem remains though: How do we account for the fact that we have unified perceptions of persistent individuals (or that Berkeley holds that we have them)? Why do I perceive 'white snow' and not 'swarming particular whites and greys and yellows, which then cease to exist when I am not perceiving them?' This is some of the work that material substances and real essences did for Locke: they provided for kinds and individuals. In denying material substances, and in affirming that the meaning of our sense experiences is how we indeed feel about them, perhaps a far more thoroughgoing scepticism was unleashed than the sort which Hylas presents.

Berkeley, unsurprisingly, brings in God to address this issue, and has Philonous remark that in order for the things that we perceive to exist when we are not perceiving them, they:

> must be in another mind . . . Now it is plain they have an existence exterior to my mind, since I find them by experience to be independent of it. There is therefore some other mind wherein they exist, during the intervals between the times of my perceiving them: As likewise they did before my birth, and would do after my supposed annihilation. And as the same is true, with regard to all other finite created spirits; it necessarily follows, there is an *omnipresent eternal Mind*, which knows and comprehends all things, and exhibits them to our view in such a manner, and according to such rules as He Himself hath ordained, and are by us termed the *Laws of Nature*. (*D* II: 230–1)

God is the omnipresent omniperceiver who holds together things, and is also the creator of the particular passive ideas which we experience through our senses. Even if we allow that Berkeley's proofs of God work by early eighteenth-century standards (Butler's objection aside), and that if God is omniscient he knows all things, there are still further problems. First, it is not clear how this is to work. God cannot have our perceptions in his mind just as we perceive them, because they are passive and God is wholly active (otherwise Berkeley's arguments against Malebranche's doctrine of seeing all things in God would lose their teeth). So what is God thinking or perceiving, and how does it unify our perceptions? On the other hand, God can't be perceiving something wholly different from our perceptions, because then our perceptions would be unperceived when we were not perceiving them – God would be perceiving something else. Also, again, it is not clear why there must be stable things when we are not perceiving them. This feels like another more refined stage of materialism, which Berkeley himself ought to shed and fully embrace a manifold of perceptions! Or to put it differently, there seems to be an unusual degree of parity between arguments against materialism and arguments against idealism.[98]

As to the last objection, Berkeley would respond we clearly do have reason to believe that there are things – stable unities – but we do not have reasons to believe that there is matter. To try to dismantle these perceptions of things is scepticism, a scepticism at odds with the rejection of matter in that there is no repugnancy in positing their continuity. The question is rather how and what they signify. Of course, one might respond that there is no reason to presume that we perceive ideas and not things either, and this was indeed the tactic taken by Thomas Reid (who was deeply influenced by Berkeley).

Berkeley's intuition is, I think, that we just do experience well-formed chunks of meaning, which on reflection do mean, and which do relate to other chunks of meaning, much as we understand a language: 'stri' and 'pe' only mean something when conjoined as 'stripe' and then 'blue stripe', and so forth. This is a powerful intuition and not obviously false, although it needs more explanation. But the other problem still remains: How and what does God 'perceive'? Berkeley is unfortunately rather scant in his explanations. Philonous says:

> And (not to mention your having discarded those archetypes) so may you suppose an external archetype on my principles; *external*, I mean, to your own mind; though indeed it must be supposed to exist in that mind which comprehends all things; but then this serves all the ends of identity, as well as if it existed out of a mind. And I am sure you yourself will not say it is less intelligible. (*D* II: 248)

This passage clearly asserts that an external archetype can serve the ends of identity, and this archetype is in the omnipresent omniperceiver's mind. Berkeley is only weakly avowing a divine archetype theory ('you may suppose'), but he allows that whatever sort of unity a thing has is due to the (presumably) active idea of the thing – as opposed to the ideas of the particular passive perceptions which we experience and from which we educe the thing – in God's mind. This passage and his use of the odd word ectypal (or sensible) has resonances of the Malbrancheian John Norris and of the Cambridge Platonist Ralph Cudworth, and passages in their work such as: 'Truths are not multiply'd by the diversity of minds, that apprehend them; because they are all but ectypal participations of one and the same original or archetypal mind and truth.'

But what (and how) exactly they are in God's mind is difficult to say. The archetype cannot be a remote unperceived ideal, because then we would have an analogous sceptical quandary, as in Books III and IV of Locke's *Essay* for Platonists. Pitcher has argued that in the *Notebooks,* Berkeley at some points seems to argue for a theory of divine powers or capacities to cause perceptions, which he then abandons – rightly – to adopt a theory where God perceives ideas, which sustains their existence, and one where he just thinks them – neither of which seems wholly appealing on either philosophical or textual grounds.[99] This exemplifies the quandary I discussed above. There are a number of passages in the *Principles* that discuss unperceived objects (notably *P* 45–8) ,but they are not decisive.

Winkler argues that this is a good example of an issue where Berkeley's thinking about religious issues is crucial for making sense of a general doctrine.[100] Berkeley seems to have accepted that ideas must be known in order to be willed, and that God cannot act as a 'blind agent'. One of the major differences between the *Dialogues* and the *Principles* is the extended discussion of creation in the former, in response to Lady Percival's objections. The problem with immaterialism for the normal Christian is not just that God makes man out of earth and breathes life into him, and this doesn't appear to be just the creation of ideas. Rather, if God knows all beings from eternity, how could they be created temporally and in order ('On the first day . . .')? Wouldn't God just always know them and they would therefore always be? The problem is serious in that here we see what appears to be a necessary role for matter – that which is created according to an archetype but is distinct from the perception of the archetype.

Philonous responds that 'I understand that the several parts of the world become gradually perceivable to finite spirits, endowed with proper faculties': i.e., it can be explained through the ordering of divine perceptions for our apprehension. But Hylas is unsatisfied and presses on Philonous to give a more orthodox response. Philonous answers:

> What would you have! do I not acknowledge a twofold state of things, the one ectypal or natural, the other archetypal and eternal? The former was created in time; the latter existed from everlasting in the mind of God. Is not this agreeable to the common notions of divines? Or is any more than this necessary in

order to conceive the Creation? But you suspect some peculiar repugnancy, though you know not where it lies. To take away all possibility of scruple in the case, do but consider this one point. Either you are not able to conceive the Creation on any hypothesis whatsoever; and if so, there is no ground for dislike or complaint against any particular opinion on that score: Or you are able to conceive it; and if so, why not on my principles, since thereby nothing conceivable is taken away? (*D* II: 254–5)

In other words, we are dealing with revealed matters, and so a problem that weighs against the immaterialist should not be decisive if it is a problem for the materialist as well. Berkeley's general solution is that our perceptions are created in time according to eternal archetypes, which are presumably active. The archetypes are what God eternally perceives in order to create, and they are presumably what gives unity to the many created perceptions, which are whatever they are insofar as they are passive, created aspects of archetypes. Since all are perceived, by us or by God, God need not perceive our particular sense perceptions in order to create them and to keep objects in existence, and He created them or revealed them (which is the same thing) in the order of creation.

Still, problems nag. If to be something is just to be a perception, how could the archetypal perception and the ectypal perception mean and be the same thing? It seems as if what we perceive (ectype/particular sense perception) is ultimately something we don't perceive but someone else does (archetype/unified and unifying object of divine thought). The Platonist language also gives pause for the hard-edged imagist.

Notions and spiritual substance (230–5)

A further question is: How and what do we know of God at all, if all of our ideas are images and God is not an image? Philonous offers a procedure reminiscent of Descartes' account of our knowledge of God in the *Third Meditation*:

I own I have properly no idea, either of God or any other spirit; for these being active, cannot be represented by things perfectly inert, as our ideas are. I do nevertheless know, that I who am a spirit or thinking substance, exist as certainly, as I know my ideas exist. Farther, I know what I mean by the terms I and *myself*; and

I know this immediately, or intuitively, though I do not perceive it as I perceive a triangle, a colour, or a sound. The mind, spirit or soul, is that *indivisible* unextended thing, which thinks, acts, and perceives. I say indivisible, because *unextended*; and unextended, because extended, figured, moveable things, are ideas; and that which perceives ideas, which thinks and wills, is plainly itself no idea, nor like an idea. Ideas are things inactive, and perceived: And spirits a sort of beings altogether different from them. I do not therefore say my soul is an idea, or like an idea. However, taking the word *idea* in a large sense, my soul can be said to furnish me with an idea, that is, an image, or likeness of God, though indeed extremely inadequate. For all the notion I have of God, is obtained by reflecting on my own soul, heightning its powers, and removing its imperfections. I have therefore, though not an inactive idea, yet in my self some sort of an active thinking image of the deity. And though I perceive him not by sense, yet I have a notion of him, or know him by reflexion and reasoning. My own mind and my own ideas I have an immediate knowledge of; and by the help of these, do mediately apprehend the possibility of the existence of other spirits and ideas. Farther, from my own being, and from the dependency I find in myself and my Ideas, I do by an act of reason, necessarily infer the existence of a God, and all created things in the mind of God. (*D* II: 231–2)

We are able to form a notion of God, and notions of other spirits or minds, through reflecting on our own actions and mental processes. As noted before, Locke argued in the *Essay* that there are two sources of knowledge: sense perception, and reflection on our own actions, faculties, and mental processes. Notions are 'ideas' of the second sort, thinking about processes not images. And unlike images, which we perceive immediately but from which we only have mediate knowledge, notions are immediate, intuitive knowledge of our own minds and our own mental processes and reasonings.

We form our notion of God by reflecting on our powers, heightening them, and then removing imperfections. We form our notions of other minds by reading external signs – blushes for example – and by reflecting on what lies behind these external signs. Consequently, that we do not have an idea or representation of God is a boon, since we have an even more immediate access. Recall the quote that began our discussion of the distinction between immediate perceptions and things signified:

> In reading a book, what I immediately perceive are the letters, but mediately, or by means of these, are suggested to my mind the notions of God, virtue, truth, &c. (*D* II: 174)

Notions can be suggested to us by immediate perceptions of letters as well as by the many other sorts of immediate sense perceptions that we have considered. But they presume a prior notion, which can only be acquired or known through direct access to and reflection on my own thoughts and mental processes. This is a further meaning of the passage from *Alciphron* where Alciphron is asked to look in the mirror to understand natural signification. Berkeley's world is about minds and spirits, and is only meaningful because of them.

This is an area of Berkeley's philosophy that Thomas Reid found to be particularly weak. Reid thought that Berkeley had packed far too much into his doctrine of perception, that we don't just have raw feels but we feel thick concepts that stock our mind, and had developed his theory of concepts far too little. In response a Berkeleyin can say that there *just is* something mysterious about any doctrine of notions: it involves the mind inspecting itself and trying to make sense of its own contents. It is immediate but doesn't involve images. And it is ongoing.

Berkeley had argued throughout the 'First Dialogue' that perceptions are mind dependent. This seemed initially to mean 'in minds'; but in the 'Third Dialogue' it became apparent that he meant that perceptions depend on minds, but are not in them even in the sense that fish are in a pond. Notions, rather, are in minds in a strong sense, or even *of* minds. The stress laid on unified mental power has a distinctly Cartesian flavour to it, as does the division between a passive reception of images that is opposed to the intuitive, immediate, and active exercise of a mind on itself: for example, in Descartes the difference between knowledge of the *cogito* and the existence of God and knowledge of images. Locke, Malebranche, and many other philosophers shared this account of unified mental power; and Malebranche shared the idea that thought is essential to the mind as opposed to sensation or imagining.[101] But unlike Berkeley's internal arguments against materialism, where he could draw on the positions of others in order to show them inconsistent, he needs to justify his positive statements about the nature of mind and ideas.

According to Berkeley, we know that we are not just a 'system of floating ideas' by the following brief argument within the long quote above:

> The mind, spirit or soul, is that *indivisible* unextended thing, which thinks, acts, and perceives. I say indivisible, because unextended; and *unextended*, because extended, figured, moveable things, are ideas; and that which perceives ideas, which thinks and wills, is plainly itself no idea, nor like an idea.

The soul must be unified because it is indivisible. It is not divisible because it is not extended: only extended things can be divided, and only ideas that are perceived by the mind but do not constitute the mind are extended. Since it is not extended it is unified. Berkeley supports this argument with the further premise:

> Ideas are things inactive, and perceived: And spirits a sort of beings altogether different from them. I do not therefore say my soul is an idea, or like an idea.

We know that ideas are passive because we can find no activity or power in them. We know we and other spirits are active from direct knowledge of our power and activity through the active inspection of our active faculties. Consequently we know that they are very different from one another (see also *P* 27)

Berkeley adds a further argument in the *Principles*:

> We perceive a continual succession of ideas, some are anew excited, others are changed or totally disappear. There is therefore some cause of these ideas, whereon they depend, and which produces and changes them. That this cause cannot be any quality or idea or combination of ideas, is clear from the preceding section. I must therefore be a substance. (*P* 26)

Sequential changes in inert ideas must be ascribable to something that can act – a substance. This argument is reminiscent of Descartes' famous discussion of the wax in the 'Second Meditation', that a thinking substance is presupposed to unify our shifting perceptions: but Berkeley is resisting Descartes' inference that general or abstract ideas are more real than particular perceptions (*PC* 784), and instead just concluding that a thinking substance is needed to unify. It seems that the substance might either be me, or God, and it might be the case that I am totally passive and God is totally active: although Berkeley concludes 'I must therefore be a substance'.

That only extension is divisible would seem to further imply that we cannot divide our mental powers at all, and when we think or will or sense each of these are modes of one and the same thinking substance (see *P* 27 in particular). This doctrine of the unity of soul or spirit pulls though against the doctrine of the heterogeneity of the senses. If each of our senses has a totally different object, and each sensing even has a different object, how can the different incommensurate senses all be one unified power? Berkeley's account of mind pulls us towards an idealism of a Christianized Platonist sort, where God thinks unified archetypical objects and we are unified minds exercising our powers in a unified manner in ways that conduce to our moral and spiritual benefit as willed and desired by God. Berkeley's account of ideas pulls us in an opposite direction, where heterogeneous senses give heterogeneous reports on a multiplicity of objects, which we then amalgamate with mysterious relations and laws of thought. The unifying power of Cartesian common sense and Cartesian general ideas is not open to him because of the denial of abstract ideas.

Hume read Berkeley and clearly learned much from him, but famously concluded in his discussion of personal identity that we are just a system or bundle of 'floating ideas', some more vivid and some less vivid. Kant sought to explain the sort of problem of Berkeley's two 'pulls' by arguing that the mind unites intuitions and concepts through a unifying, noumenal self. For Berkeley – much more than for Hume and Kant – behind these questions about the unity and disparity of mind are moral and religious issues captured by his shifting use of 'spirit', 'soul', and 'mind' (a shifting use that was perfectly ordinary in the period in which he wrote).

Action, good and evil (236–7)
For example, if we are continuously being presented with ideas by God, and there is nothing beside our perceptions and the notions we form about ourselves and others, how can we act? This seems a basic

problem with Berkeley's account: it denies action. The unity of spirit means that the will is just a mode of the mind:

> A spirit is one simple, undivided, active being – as it perceives ideas it is called the understanding, and as it produces or other-wise operates about them it is called the will. Hence there can be no idea formed of a soul or spirit; for all ideas whatever, being passive and inert (vide sect. 25), they cannot represent unto us, by way of image or likeness, that which acts. A little attention will make it plain to any one, that to have an idea which shall be like that active principle of motion and change of ideas is absolutely impossible. Such is the nature of spirit, or that which acts, that it cannot be of itself perceived, but only by the effects which it produceth. (*P* 27)

Given that Berkeley was the author or 'Passive Obedience', it is not terribly surprising that he might deny action! Perhaps there really is no room for action in Berkeley's theory, and that's that.[102] It is notable that Berkeley alludes to a very strong deontic moral theory in the 'Third Dialogue'. Hylas criticizes Philonous for making God the direct author of evil by making him the direct of author of all of our perceptions. Philonous points out that this is a theodicy problem that holds of any theory: whether God acts directly or by an instrument, He is still responsible for His acts. Philonous then goes on:

> I farther observe, that sin or moral turpitude doth not consist in the outward physical action or motion, but in the internal devi-ation of the will from the laws of reason and religion. This is plain, in that the killing an enemy in a battle, or putting a crimi-nal legally to death, is not thought sinful, though the outward act be the very same with that in the case of murder. Since therefore sin doth not consist in the physical action, the making God an immediate cause of all such actions, is not making him the author of sin. Lastly, I have no where said that God is the only agent who produces all the motions in bodies. It is true, I have denied there are any other agents besides spirits: But this is very consistent with allowing to thinking rational beings, in the pro-duction of motions, the use of limited powers, ultimately indeed derived from God, but immediately under the direction of their

own wills, which is sufficient to entitle them to all the guilt of their actions. (*D* II: 236–7)

Here Philonous seems to be both biting the bullet of volitionalism (that we can have volitions on the basis of which we can act, but not physical actions),[103] and allowing spirits some use of limited powers of action. What these 'limited powers' could be is truly mysterious. He certainly would want us to be morally responsible for our habits and dispositions, and he would doubtless argue that our capacities to imagine, to think or not to think, and to attend to or not attend to are the ground for subsequent dispositions on which we can be judged. That we are unified spirits allows for a unified moral judgment (as opposed to 'I'll give you a ten for your thinking but a two for your willing'). But here he says in addition that we can produce motion in a limited way.

He might have in mind that we can dispose our body in different ways to receive and respond to sensations.[104] As we discussed earlier, there is a gap in Berkeley's theory of perception between passive perception and active thinking – bodily motion. This gap seems the likely candidate for 'limited powers'. Through this capacity we can turn towards the fruit on a tree, a cherry or a forbidden fruit, turn away, and be judged. It alters how and what we perceive, but in a restricted way: we cannot turn to inspect a crater on the moon if we are in a cave beneath the surface of the earth. And, the ability to use the capacity rests on prior use (how did we end up in that cave anyway?).

I have little doubt that this is what Berkeley is suggesting: that Berkeley thinks that this alters perceptions but does not initiate causal sequences, and that this explains the two tendencies in the passage above. *Pace* T.S. Eliot, it is because I do hope to turn again that God judges me. But, there would still need to be some further explanation of how this limited capacity can influence perception. Are there always multiple perceptions that might be available to me, but God exhibits particular perceptions to me on the basis of how I have turned? Does this mean that God is then involved in a massive coordination problem of perceptions, much like Leibniz's God is in the *Monadology*? But God is omniscient, so he must have foreknowledge of how I will turn.

Berkeley would respond that these are problems for the materialist and dualist as well, and nothing specific to immaterialism. It is ironic that in discussing Berkeley on action, as opposed to Berkeley on notions, we encounter problems of reconciling necessity and agency, problems we often associate with a compatabilist theory that leans heavily on materialist explanations. Sometimes Berkeley suggests that immaterialism will dissolve all philosophical problems; but in the 'Third Dialogue' he more often admits that there are issues that immaterialism does not have a more special purchase on than the other contenders. It just leads to fewer repugnances and so is to be preferred.

Gravity (262–3)

The *Three Dialogues* conclude with a wonderful image of a fountain:

> You see, Hylas, the water of yonder fountain, how it is forced upwards, in a round column, to a certain height; at which it breaks and falls back into the basin from whence it rose: Its ascent as well as descent, proceeding from the same uniform law or principle of *gravitation*. Just so, the same principles which at first view lead to *scepticism*, pursued to a certain point, bring men back to common sense. (*D* II: 262–3)

We are in the garden and Hylas' aggressive scepticism has given way to a greater calm as he has accepted the immaterialist philosophy. Seeing the world aright has set Hylas aright, one of Berkeley's major points. He is no longer agitated or irritable, and presumably with his mind now at rest he will go to bed at a decent hour and wake up at a decent hour as well. The passage I have just quoted is in response to Hylas' statement:

> I have been a long time distrusting my senses; methought I saw things by a dim light, and through false glasses. Now the glasses are removed, and a new light breaks in upon my understanding. I am clearly convinced that I see things in their native forms; and am no longer in pain about their unknown natures or absolute existence. This is the state I find my self in at present: though indeed the course that brought me to it, I do not yet thoroughly comprehend. You set out upon the same principles that Academics, Cartesians, and the like sects, usually do; and for a long time it looked as if you were advancing their philosophical *scepticism*; but in the end your conclusions are directly opposite to theirs. (*D* II: 262)

The image of gravity would, of course, have raised the spectre of Newton in his reader's minds. Berkeley is not denying gravity, nor denying the uniformity of the law or principle of gravitation. He is instead challenging the philosophical presuppositions and inferences of those who worshipped the discovery of the law of gravity as *the* great accomplishment of early modern natural philosophy, claiming them to be unwarranted, and further asking what is lost if we adopt these pictures. The removal of false glasses – presumably representing our philosophical presumptions about matter that distort and stain how and what we see – results in clear sight. We can now enjoy the fountain.

As we have seen at various points, Berkeley was actively engaged with Newton's discoveries – both as natural philosopher and as mathematician – for much of his career. He often viewed himself as saving Newton's discoveries from his advocates, such as Samuel Clarke, and from his own bad metaphysical tendencies. The image of the fountain is preceded by a lengthy discussion of all of the areas of inquiry that are to be improved by immaterialism, including natural philosophy:

> In natural philosophy, what intricacies, what obscurities, what contradictions, hath the belief of matter led men into! To say nothing of the numberless disputes about its extent, continuity, homogeneity, gravity, divisibility, &c. do they not pretend to explain all things by bodies operating on bodies, according to the laws of motion? and yet, are they able to comprehend how one body should move another? Nay, admitting there was no difficulty in reconciling the notion of an inert being with a cause; or in conceiving how an accident might pass from one body to another; yet by all their strained thoughts and extravagant suppositions, have they been able to reach the mechanical production of any one animal or vegetable body? Can they account by the laws of motion, for sounds, tastes, smells, or colours, or for the regular course of things? Have they accounted by physical principles for the aptitude and contrivance, even of the most inconsiderable parts of the universe? But laying aside matter and corporeal causes, and admitting only the efficiency of an all–perfect mind, are not all the effects of nature easy and intelligible? If the phænomena are nothing else but *ideas*; God is a *spirit*, but matter an unintelligent, unperceiving being. If they demonstrate

an unlimited power in their cause; God is active and omnipotent, but matter an inert mass. If the order, regularity, and usefulness of them, can never be sufficiently admired; God is infinitely wise and provident, but matter destitute of all contrivance and design. These surely are great advantages in *physics*. Not to mention that the apprehension of a distant Deity, naturally disposes men to a negligence in their *moral* actions, which they would be more cautious of, in case they thought Him immediately present, and acting on their minds without the interposition of matter, or unthinking second causes. (*D* II: 257–8)

Berkeley is offering immaterialism as an alternative theoretical backing for Newton's discoveries. It does not fall into the errors of abstract ideas, it does not remove God and apparently deny incarnation[105] or qualitative properties and signs from the world, or damn up the chunks of meaning that we naturally encounter in our ordinary experience, yet at the same time it does not wholly disturb rational explanations of phenomena. Gravity still is a regular force and regularly describable according to natural laws; but we shouldn't think that the laws describe metaphysically real abstract properties, whether gravity or motion. Of course, given all the worries we have discussed about holism, individuating properties and qualities and so on, how Berkeley's theory was to work is a difficult (or perhaps impossible) question, although it is clear that his theory is instrumentalist and interpretive, not absolute and abstract.

But the passage says something additional:

Its ascent as well as descent, proceeding from the same uniform law or principle of *gravitation*. Just so, the same principles which at first view lead to *scepticism*, pursued to a certain point, bring men back to common sense. (*D* II: 263)

The law of gravity is in addition an analogy for something else: the rise to scepticism and the fall back to common sense. Both have the same source – reason – and scepticism must fall back to common sense because it is an endeavour of reasoners, but one which cannot coherently support itself. And of course the water in a font will suggest further analogies, of life and more. On Berkeley's account physical laws are not links between mute bodies within a container, but rather meaning producers and happiness and goodness acquirers.

Since all perceptions are created by God, every perception is chosen and meaningful in some sense for those who wish to read. And they produce further meaning through reading and interpretation. Shortly after Berkeley this attempt to reconcile science and the endless meaningfulness and endless interpretability of nature would come under a different attack, inspired in part by Berkeley, from the side of those who argued against science and mathematics and for beauty and interpretation. In Berkeley we see one of the most interesting attempts to draw them together.

And, given that the *Three Dialogues* is a book, we are reading words, and taken together they mean, and allow us to engage in a dialogue, it seems a fitting ending.

QUESTIONS

1. Are you now a convinced immaterialist? Why not? Are these good reasons or are you just stubborn?
2. Do we really have direct knowledge of the fact that we are an active spirit? Isn't this in fact heavily mediated knowledge (by society, by other experiences, by our upbringing, and so on)? (This question is a variant on what philosophers following Sellars sometimes refer to as the 'Myth of the Given'.)
3. Is a Berkeley without God meaningful or supportable? How?

CHAPTER FOUR

RECEPTION AND INFLUENCE

The influence of the *Three Dialogues* is difficult to separate from the influence of Berkeley's philosophical works more generally. The *Three Dialogues* may have been a specific influence on Hume when he wrote in the dialogue form, but in general philosophers have (mostly rightly) contracted the *Principles* and the *Three Dialogues* into one doctrine. Consequently I will briefly discuss the influence of both. These are really just suggestions to the reader of philosophers they might look to who had interesting and influential engagements with Berkeley.

As was noted at the outset, the *Principles* and the *Three Dialogues* were not smashing successes. As the eighteenth century elapsed, more philosophers took Berkeley's doctrines into account and more seriously, in particular in Scotland. As discussed throughout, Hume seems to have been deeply and pervasively influenced by Berkeley (along with Bayle, Malebranche, Mandeville, Hutcheson, Locke, Butler, Shaftesbury, and many others!). This can be seen most strongly in 'Scepticism of the Senses', but also in his use of 'vivacity' to differentiate between ideas, in his adoption of a *minima* theory in his account of space, in his instrumental explanation of 'abstract' ideas, in his tendencies towards emotivism, and many, many other areas of his philosophy. Indeed 'Locke, Berkeley, Hume' was *the* orthodoxy in discussing eighteenth-century British philosophers, until historians of philosophy began to fill out the picture and consider the many other influences on Hume as well. But the fact that real history is considerably more complicated than retrospective conceptual genealogy should not diminish the importance of Berkeley's influence on Hume.

That said, Hume's basic strategy is to take over a Berkeleyin argument or a Berkeleyin criticism and then to argue for a sceptical position as resulting from the opposition between Berkeley's arguments and the standard position. Berkeley would certainly have been scandalized that his doctrines were ferment not for love of God or decent morality, but for deeper and deeper scepticism and atheism. Many today would consider Hume's arguments one of Berkeley's greatest accomplishments, in that he is a major source of their style, rigour and cleverness.

The triumvirate 'Locke, Berkeley, Hume' was due above all to Immanuel Kant and Thomas Reid. Both offered pictures of the history of philosophy as the history of epistemology, in which Locke put forth a realist program that was then challenged by Berkeley, turned into a sceptical morass by Hume, and reconciled and solved by them! Kant considered Berkeley as an example of 'subjective idealism', which allowed him to develop his own 'transcendental idealism'. We can see strong influence of a Berkeleyan problem in Kant, perhaps via Hume. For example: 'What gives unity and substantiality to my floating system of ideas?' Reid relatedly criticized Berkeley as one of the major exponents of the theory of ideas, and argued that scepticism was the result not of materialism but of interposing ideas between us and an inaccessible reality that the ideas signify – the so-called 'veil of perception'. One needed to get rid not just of matter, but of ideas, to avoid scepticism.

That being said, Berkeley was an enormous influence on Reid. Reid's arguments that we directly perceive things, that the doctrine of representation results in a destructive two-world hypothesis, and that more teleology must be brought into the modern view to make sense of it in opposition to the early modern mechanist picture of nature are all very influenced by Berkeley. Reid's earliest work, *An Inquiry into the Human Mind on the Principles of Common Sense* (1764), explores each of the senses in a fashion highly reminiscent of Berkeley, making heavy use of Berkeley's account of vision, and with references to Berkeley throughout. There is an extended, uncharitable, and (unfortunately) influential discussion of Berkeley's philosophy in Reid's later *Essays on the Intellectual Powers of Man* (1785), which tended to be how Berkeley was read by many in the nineteenth century. But Reid's debt to Berkeley was as large (or larger) than to any other philosopher.

Berkeley met and corresponded with an American philosopher named Samuel Johnson (not the British stone kicker), and their exchanges are lively and philosophically rich (II:267–94). Johnson was convinced by immaterialism, published a Berkeley-inspired work called *Elementa Philosophica* (1752) (printed by Benjamin Franklin), and authored textbooks. The works proved to be popular: Johnson was influential on the nascent American educational system, and immaterialism found a home in the New World despite the collapse of the 'Bermuda Project'. The influence of Berkeley, in particular his instrumentalist attitude towards general ideas and his stress on signification, can be seen on the greatest eighteenth-century American philosopher, Charles Saunders Peirce, who declared Berkeley his greatest influence (granted, along with a number of other philosophers!).

The German philosopher and theologian Johann Gerrg Hamann was deeply influenced by Berkeley. Through him Berkeley's stress of language, interpretation and holism had a continuing influence on post-Kantian German philosophy. Hamann also drew on Berkeley's 'divine language'. This is in his path-breaking criticisms of Kant. In the nineeenth century, John Stuart Mill was deeply influenced in his *Logic* by what he considered to be Berkeley's phenomenalism, as well as by the rigour of his descriptions of phenomenal experiences. In the early twentieth century Berkeley's ideas were taken up by Bertrand Russell, and then by Ayer and the logical positivists. This was a Berkeley centred on the *New Theory of Vision*: not Berkeley the theological teleologist but Berkeley the rigorist describer of sense experience. The 'sense datum' theory was also often coupled with an equally Berkeley-inspired emotivist theory of ethics – that ethical propositions are reports of feelings. To present Berkeley as solely a 'sense datum' theorist is to do him a disservice: but this tendency is there in him as well as emotivism (influencing Ayer, Charles Stevenson and many others). Whether they can be decoupled from God and still be meaningful is a different question!

Berkeley the teleologist and immaterialist inspired British, Scottish, and American idealists – most notably F.H. Bradley – and was a sensible, native British voice incorporated into their modified Hegelianisms. It is interesting to think of the battle between British idealism and logical positivism as a battle between two Berkeleys. It is clear which Berkeley won.

There are still very able defenders of idealism today, notably Howard Robinson, John Foster, and Timothy Sprigge. This is a minority position. But Berkeley's style of argument, his attention to perception, and his arguments themselves have very much become the majority.

CHAPTER FIVE

GUIDE TO FURTHER READING

There are many good books on Berkeley's philosophy. I have cited some of the works that have particularly influenced me throughout this book. This is a much more limited list, where I will list a few suggestions for further reading. There will obviously be many good books on Berkeley that are not on this list: and the fact that they do not appear here should not be taken as a sign of disapproval.

1. FIRST PLACE TO LOOK

Winkler, K.J. (ed.), *The Cambridge Companion to Berkeley* (Cambridge: Cambridge University Press, 2005).
A clear, state of the art, and edifying collection with an exhaustive bibliography.

2. GENERAL STUDIES ON THE 'THREE DIALOGUES'

Stoneham, T., *Berkeley's World: An Examination of the Three Dialogues* (Oxford: Oxford University Press, 2003).
This is an excellent, detailed treatment of Berkeley's arguments.

3. BACKGROUND MATERIAL

McCracken, C.J. and Tipton, I.C., *Berkeley's Principles and Dialogues: Background Source Materials* (Cambridge: Cambridge University, 2000).
Collects passages from many of the authors I have discussed as influencing Berkeley, along with early reviews and other interesting texts.

4. GENERAL STUDIES ON BERKELEY

Grayling, A.C., *Berkeley: The Central Arguments* (London: Duckworth, 1986).

Pitcher, G., *Berkeley* (London: Routledge & Kegan Paul, 1977).

Tipton, I., *Berkeley: The Philosophy of Immaterialism* (London: Methuen, 1974).

Winkler, K.J., *Berkeley: An Interpretation* (Oxford: Oxford University Press, 1989).

All major studies. These are good places to start.

5. ON VISION

Atherton, M., *Berkeley's Revolution in Vision* (Ithaca: Cornell University Press, 1990).

The now standard work.

6. ON NOTIONS

Flage, D., *Berkeley's Doctrine of Notions: A Reconstruction Based on His Theory of Meaning* (London: Croom Helm, 1987).

Difficult but fascinating.

7. ON RELIGION

Berman, D., *George Berkeley: Idealist and the Man* (Oxford: Clarendon Press, 1994).

Also a biography.

8. ON RHETORIC

Walmsley, P., *The Rhetoric of Berkeley's Philosophy* (Cambridge: Cambridge University Press, 1990).

9. COLLECTIONS

Muehlmann, R.G. (ed.), *Berkeley's Metaphysics: Structural Interpretive and Critical Essays* (State College, PA: Penn State Press, 1995).

Turbayne, C. (ed.), *Berkeley: Critical and Interpretive Essays*
(Minneapolis: University of Minneapolis Press, 1982)

NOTES

1: CONTEXT

1 'What Berkeley discovered was that material things must be definable in terms of sense contents . . . The unfortunate thing is that, in spite of this, he found it necessary to postulate God as an unobservable cause of our "ideas".' A.J. Ayer, *Language, Truth and Logic* (New York: Dover, 1952), p. 53.

2 J.L. Austin, *Sense and Sensibilia* (Oxford: Oxford University Press, 1962), pp. 132–42. G.J. Warnock, *Berkeley* (Oxford: Blackwell, 1982), pp. 225–35.

3 For a brilliant discussion of this theme as it relates to Locke and Berkeley, see Margaret Dauler Wilson, 'History of Philosophy in Philosophy Today; and the Case of Sensible Qualities', *Philosophical Review* 101:1 (1992), pp. 191–243.

4 Archbishop William King, who was a philosophical influence on Francis Hutcheson and on Christian utilitarianism through his work *De Origine Mali*, had Berkeley prosecuted in episcopal court for failing to remain a deacon for an appropriate length of time before his promotion to the higher office of priest. Nothing came of the prosecution. See M.A. Stewart, 'George Berkeley' in the *Dictionary of National Biography*.

5 This entry has a '+' next to it in the margins of the notebook. All the entries in Berkeley's *Notebooks* have marginal annotations — symbols ('x', '+', '*', etc.), letters ('I', 'N'), multiple letters ('M.S.', 'S.E.', 'Mo'), and abbreviated words ('Introd' for 'Introduction'). Sometimes there are multiple annotations ('X +'). The meanings of many of the annotations are clear, but in a few cases the meaning is highly disputed. In particular, '+' appears to signify a philosophical position that Berkeley has given up, but Berkeley does not appear to use it consistently. See Robert McKim, 'Berkeley's Notebooks' in Ken Winkler (ed.), *The Cambridge Companion to Berkeley* (Cambridge: Cambridge University Press, 2005), pp. 63–93.

6 Richard Steele, the famous author of the *Spectator*, apparently sought Berkeley's company after having read the *Principles* ('Letter

To Percival, London, Feb. 23rd, 1712/13' *Berkeley's Works,* VIII, p. 61).

7 'After we came out of the church, we stood talking for some time together of Bishop Berkeley's ingenious sophistry to prove the non-existence of matter, and that every thing in the universe is merely ideal. I observed, that though we are satisfied his doctrine is not true, it is impossible to refute it. I never shall forget the alacrity with which Johnson answered, striking his foot with mighty force against a large stone, till he rebounded from it, "I refute it THUS."' Boswell, *Life of Johnson* (1763).

8 'In 1985 . . . David Stove ran a Competition to Find the Worst Argument in the World. In his marking scheme, half the marks went to the degree of badness of the argument, half to the degree of its endorsement by philosophers. Thus an argument was sought that was both very bad, and very prevalent. He awarded the prize to himself, for the following argument. '"We can know things only as they are related to us . . . So, we cannot know things as they are in themselves". . . . Stove himself was most concerned with this argument as it occurred in classical idealism. Berkeley argued "the mind . . . is deluded to think it can and does conceive of bodies existing unthought of, or without the mind, though at the same time they are apprehended by, or exist in, itself." That is, "you cannot have trees-without-the-mind in mind, without having them in mind. Therefore, you cannot have trees-without-the-mind in mind." This argument, which Stove called "the Gem", is a version of the "Worst Argument" because it argues from the fact that we can know physical things only under our own mental forms to the impossibility of knowing physical things at all.' James Franklin, 'Stove's Discovery of the Worst Argument in the World,' *Philosophy* 77 (2002) 615–16. Of course, Stove's version of Berkeley's argument is questionable. To be fair to Stove, he is more interested in the genealogy of a bad argument than in Berkeley.

9 The manuscript was lost at sea on the way to Naples in 1713 (II: 282).

10 Nearly 30 years later this scene was replayed when David Hume recast the content of the poorly received *A Treatise of Human Nature* (1739–40) in the two *Enquiries* (1753).

11 Through the *Dialogues* Berkeley did have his first high-ranking convert: Dr Arbuthnot, the Queen's physician and well-known writer. 'This Dr Arbuthnot is the first proselyte I have made by the Treatise I came over to print, which will soon be published' ('Letter to Percival, London, Apr. 16th, 1713,' *Berkeley's Works* IX, p .65).

12 See Lisa Downing, 'Berkeley's Natural Philosophy and Philosophy of Science' in *Cambridge Companion to Berkeley,* p. 236.

13 Like many British philosophers and clergymen, Berkeley had a keen sense for the distinctions between different 'confessions' or types of Christianity. The Church of England or Anglican Church was the state church established by Henry VIII, with a church hierarchy headed by the British monarch. There was a strongly religious element to the conflict in the English Civil War and it continued as a tension in British

society. Those who did not subscribe to the creed or 'articles' of the Anglican Church and practised another brand of Protestantism (of which there were many types, from hardline Presbyterians in Scotland to Unitarians in America) were called 'dissenters'. Since one had to subscribe to the articles of the Church of England in order to go to Oxford, Cambridge, or Trinity in Dublin, the dissenters set up their own schools called 'dissenting academies' in England, and they emigrated to places highly tolerant of dissent (like Rhode Island). Needless to say Berkeley must have felt surrounded by the enemy!

14 Bernard Mandeville (1670–1733) was a Leiden-trained physician, a pioneering psychiatrist, and author, best known for his work *The Fable of the Bees*, which was first published in 1714 but became notorious in the 1720s, when it went through a succession of expanding editions. The subtitle of the work was 'Private Vices, Public Virtues', and Mandeville (sometimes called 'Man-Devil' by his enemies) became associated with the doctrine that individual vices can lead to the public good. He was a major influence on David Hume and Adam Smith, and a ferocious and funny polemicist, who was occasionally brought up on public indecency charges for his writing but was protected by his good friend and dining companion Lord Macclesfield, the Lord Chancellor of England.

15 A.A. Luce, *The Life of George Berkeley Bishop of Cloyne* (London: Thomas Nelson, 1949), p. 13. The subtitle of *Siris* is: 'a chain of philosophical reflexions and inquiries concerning the virtues of tar water.'

16 Anthony Ashley Cooper (Lord Shaftesbury) (1671–1713) was one of the dominant figures in British letters in the early seventeenth century. His grandfather was the powerful opponent of James II and patron of John Locke, who served as Shaftesbury's tutor. His mother was Lady Masham, the daughter of the Cambridge Platonist Ralph Cudworth. His strange and sprawling work *Characteristicks*, with its attempt to remake ancient moral philosophy in a way that fit with contemporary mores and institutions, as well as the image of Shaftesbury as the witty, hermetic, romantic nobleman who died far too young, influenced many of the leading lights of the eighteenth century in France, Germany, England, Scotland, and further afield. For a sense of Shaftesbury's importance and influence see Isabel Rivers, *Reason, Grace, and Sentiment, A Study of the Language of Religion and Ethics in England 1660–1780* (Cambridge: Cambridge University Press, 2000), v. II.

17 Berkeley arranged to meet Malebranche in Paris 1713. See Letter 39 (*L* VIII: 74).

18 See *Spectator* 10.

19 Berkeley referred to coffeehouse wits as 'minute philosophers', as opposed to the more common 'free thinkers', in order not to give them the positive association of 'free'. 'Free thinker' was often used synonymously with 'Socinian', and 'atheist' to mean irreligious.

20 'Alciphron', one of the four main characters of Berkeley's *Alciphron, or the Minute Philosopher*, represents Shaftesbury as well as Anthony Collins and others (perhaps Hutcheson). But the character is primarily

associated with Shaftesbury. Another character, 'Lysicles', is a vulgar Epicurean who justifies himself with arguments from Mandeville. Alciphron, unlike Lysicles, is presented by Berkeley as thoughtful and serious, even if he shows himself in the end to be a sceptic.

21 But see *Passive Obedience* 22.

22 As he remarked, very characteristically, at the conclusion of *De Motu*: 'In physics sense and experience which react only to apparent effects hold sway: in mechanics the abstract notions of mathematicians are admitted. In first philosophy or metaphysics we are concerned with incorporeal things, with causes, truth, and the existence of things . . . Only by meditation and reasoning can truly active causes be rescued from the surrounding darkness and be to some extent known. To deal with them is the business of first philosophy or metaphysics. Allot to each science its own province; assign its bounds' (*DM* 71–2).

23 William Molyneux was a great influence on Berkeley's intellectual milieu, and one of the main ambassadors of Lockeanism and modern philosophy in Dublin. Berkeley dedicated one of his earliest works, 'Miscellanea Mathematica' (1707), to Samuel Molyneux: 'Filio Viri Clarissimi Gulielmi Molyneux'. See M.A. Stewart, *DNB*.

24 By this I mean a unifying faculty of the imagination or mental power connecting different ideas of sense. Not to be confused with common sense as used in the phrase: 'Don't juggle knives! You are clearly lacking in common sense!'

25 Some of the highlights are William Cheselden's account of an experiment removing the cataracts from a young man born blind in 'An account of some observations made by a young gentleman' (1728), which philosophers plumbed (inconclusively) for empirical confirmation of their answers to Molyneux's challenge; to Leibniz's argument in the *New Essays on Human Understanding* (1704/64) that a great blind mathematician like Nicholas Saunderson, the Lucasian Professor at Cambridge and friend of Newton, might be better able to distinguish the difference between a sphere and a cube than someone lacking mathematical skills or genius; Denis Diderot's *Letter on the Blind* (1749), where he argued both that the experiment was impossible to carry out and that if one accepted a hardline empiricism then the blind, since they lack certain fundamental ideas, will likely have a different morality than the sighted (landing Diderot in the Bastille); and more recently Gareth Evans' intriguing discussion ('Molyneux's question' in A. Phillips (ed.) *The Collected Papers of Gareth Evans* (Oxford: Oxford University Press, 1985)).

26 See the early reviews collected in C.J. McCracken and I.C. Tipton, *Berkeley's Principles and Dialogues: Background Source Materials* (Cambridge: Cambridge University, 2000), pp. 173–90.

27 See A.A. Luce, *Berkeley and Malebranche* (Oxford: Oxford University Press, 1934); C.J. McCracken, *Malebranche and British Philosophy* (Oxford: Clarendon Press, 1983); and Harry M. Bracken, *Berkeley* (New York: St Martin's Press, 1974).

28 John Norris (1657–1711) was best known for his Malebranche-inspired work *An Essay towards the Theory of the Ideal or Intelligible World* (1701–04), 2 v. He influenced, among others, Mary Astell.

29 For an excellent discussion see Andrew Pyle, *Malebranche* (London: Routledge, 2003), Ch. 3.

30 There is a great deal of disagreement about what Descartes really meant. See Descartes, 'Letters to Mersenne [April 15, May 6, and May 27, 1630]', in Roger Ariew (ed.), *Rene Descartes: Philosophical Essays and Correspondence* (Indianapolis: Hackett, 2000), p. 28 (*AT* I:143–53).

31 When I use the word 'content' I generally mean 'semantic content' or stuff-we-acquire-in-perception-which-means-something. When I use 'object' I use it in a very loose way to signify that which our mind is directed towards. An idea can be an object. I do not mean to suggest any tacit technical (or phenomenological) distinction between object and content by my terminology.

32 Nicolas Malebranche, *Dialogues on Metaphysics and Religion*, Nicholas Jolley and David Scott (eds and trans.), (Cambridge: Cambridge University Press, 1997), 141–2.

33 'Elucidation 6,' Nicolas Malebranche, *The Search after Truth*, Thomas J. Lennon and Paul Olscamp (eds), (Cambridge: Cambridge University Press, 1997), 575.

34 When discussing Berkeley I will use 'mind dependent' to mean dependent on a perceiver. I will use 'mind independent' to mean existing without a perceiver.

35 See particularly Malebranche, *The Search after Truth*, pp. 510–26 (VI.2.9).

36 'When I see one ball strike another, my eyes tell me, or seem to tell me, that the one is truly the cause of the motion it impresses on the other, for the true cause that moves bodies does not appear to my eyes. But when I consult my reason I clearly see that since bodies cannot move themselves, and since their motor force is but the will of God that conserves them successively in different places, they cannot communicate a power they do not have and could not communicate even if it were in their possession. For the mind will never conceive that one body, a purely passive substance, can in any way transmit to another body the power transporting it.' 'Elucidation Fifteen' in Malebranche, *Search after Truth*, p. 660.

37 Ibid, 446 (VI.2.3).

NOTES TO CHAPTER 3

1 Berkeley mentions Bayle twice in the *Notebooks* (§358, §424), in conjunction with Malebranche, making it difficult to gauge exactly what he read by Bayle.

2 'Since it is a truth evident by the light of nature, that there is a sovereign omniscient Spirit, who alone can make us for ever happy, or for ever miserable; it plainly follows that conformity to His will, and not

any prospect of temporal advantage, is the sole rule whereby every man who acts up to the principles of reason must govern and square his actions' (*PO* §6).

3 Sextus Empiricus, *Outlines of Pyrrhonism* I.x.

4 Sometimes in the arguments between Hylas and Philonous one feels a bit of internal debate between two Berkeleys. But this is uncommon.

5 Fontenelle (1657–1757) was a central figure in French intellectual society of the late seventeenth and early to mid-eighteenth century. He was best known for the *Conversations*; the *Eloges* (or obituaries) he wrote as secretary of the Académie des Sciences, which were crucial in the popularizing and spread of scientific ideas in France; and the wonderful *New Dialogues of the Dead* (1683/4), where he imagined conversations between philosophers and intellectuals from different periods of history. Along with Bayle and Shaftesbury, his work set the tone in many ways for the Enlightenment, and he was admired by many of its central figures, including Voltaire (who both celebrated and mocked him), Montesquieu (his friend), and Diderot and the Encyclopedists.

6 For example: 'The day doesn't inspire sadness and passion like the night, when everything seems to be at rest. We imagine that the stars move more quietly than the sun; everything is softer in starlight; we can fix our eyes more comfortably on the heavens; our thoughts are freer because we're so foolish as to imagine ourselves the only ones abroad to dream. Besides, in daylight we see nothing but sun and blue sky, but the night gives us all the profusion of stars in a thousand different designs, stirring as many pleasantly confused thoughts in us.' Bernard le Bovier de Fontenelle, *Conversations on the Plurality of Worlds*, H.A. Hargreaves (trans.), (Berkeley, CA: University of California Press, 1990), p. 10.

7 '"I hold it in much higher regard," she answered, "now that I know it's like a watch; it's superb that, wonderful as it is, the whole order of nature is based upon such simple things."' Ibid., p. 12.

8 Nicolas Malebranche, *Dialogues on Metaphysics and Religion*, Nicholas Jolley and David Scott (eds and trans.), (Cambridge: Cambridge University Press, 1997), p. 3–4.

9 They were highly controversial sermons, and Berkeley apparently published them to countervene charges of Jacobitism. 'Jacobitism' meant support for absolute monarchical rule and opposition to the 'right to rebellion' associated with the Glorious Revolution of 1688/9. William King, the archbishop who had opposed Berkeley's rapid promotion to priest, was a strong advocate of the Glorious Revolution, and so the accusation was particularly politically fraught. The issue came to a head in Scotland with the Jacobite Rebellion of 1745. For the historical background see David Berman, 'The Jacobitism of Berkeley's Passive Obedience', *Journal of the History of Ideas* 47:2 (1986), 309–19.

10 Anthony Ashley Cooper (Earl of Shaftesbury), *Characteristicks of Men, Manners, Opinions, Times* (Indianapolis: Liberty Fund, 2001), I: 66.

11 A good example of this sort of use is from Lewis Theobald's *Life and Character of Cato* (1713), a brief redaction and updating of classical sources on the virtuous Roman citizen published after the great success of Addison's *Cato,* intended to allow readers and viewers of the play to have a richer understanding of the background. 'The Noise immediately brought his Sons and Friends into the Chamber, on whom looking sternly, he ask'd them, *If they had observed him to have lost his common Sense?* And why they did not try to persuade him by Reasons?' (p. 22). Berkeley attended the play's premiere with Addison, and admired it (L 31, VIII: 112).

12 Shaftesbury, *Characteristicks*, I: 83. Shaftesbury's point turns out to be far more subtle than it first appears. He is interested in what makes speech or writing *appear* objective and why we judge testimony as well founded.

13 There are also obvious objections, beginning with: How do you know that you have examined enough consequences to stop and render a verdict? Couldn't the most absurd consequence always be waiting around the corner?

14 Whether grammar is arbitrary in this same sense is a matter of great dispute!

15 Reid continues: 'It may be observed that as the first class of natural signs I have mentioned, is the foundation of true philosophy, and the second, the foundation of fine arts: so the last is the foundation of common sense; a part of human nature which hath never been explained.' Thomas Reid, *An Inquiry into the Human Mind on the Principles of Common Sense*, Derek Brookes (ed.) (Edinburgh: Edinburgh University Press, 1997), 59–61 (V.4.6).

16 cf. Michael Ayers, *Locke: Epistemology and Ontology* (London: Routledge, 1991), v. I, pp. 60–6.

17 George Dicker distinguishes between an epistemic sense of immediate perception and a psychological sense of immediate perception, identifying the former (epistemological) with knowing 'its existence and nature solely on the basis of one's present perceptual experience', and the latter (psychological) as 'perceived without (the perceiver's) performing any (conscious) inference' (George Dicker, 'The Concept of Immediate Perception in Berkeley's Immaterialism' in Colin Turbayne (ed.), *Berkeley: Critical and Interpretive Essays* (Minneapolis: University of Minneapolis Press, 1982), p. 49). Dicker argues that Berkeley conflates these two senses of immediate perception, presuming that the psychological sense implies the epistemic sense, leading him to believe that many arguments go through which clearly do not when the distinction is drawn carefully. Dicker's psychological immediate perception would correspond to the experience of the sign, whereas epistemic immediate perception would involve what it is a sign of or for. Berkeley thinks much confusion arises from what we think we know of an immediate perception's existence or nature on the basis of our present perceptual experience (to paraphrase Dicker).

18 See, for starters, Douglas Greenlee, 'Locke's Idea of Idea' in I.C. Tipton (ed.), *Locke on Human Understanding* (Oxford: Oxford University Press, 1977), pp. 41–7; John Yolton, *Perceptual Acquaintance from Descartes to Reid* (Minneapolis: University of Minnesota Press, 1984), *passim*; Ayers, *Locke: Epistemology and Ontology*, v. I part 1; Vere Chappell, 'Locke's Theory of Ideas' in Vere Chappell (ed.), *The Cambridge Companion to Locke* (Cambridge: Cambridge University Press, 1994), Ch. 2.

19 John Cottingham, Robert Stoothoff, and Dugald Murdoch (eds), *The Philosophical Writings of Descartes* (Cambridge: Cambridge University Press, 1984), v. II, pp. 29–30 (*AT* VII: 43–4). Arnauld criticized Descartes' use of materially false ideas in his 'Objections' to the *Meditations* (ibid, 145–6 (AT VII206–8)). He later entered into a major controversy with Malebranche as to whether ideas are mental activity (my activity as a thinking substance) or objects of intentions (the red which I perceive). On Arnauld's controversy with Malebranche, see Pyle, *Malebranche*, Ch. 4.

20 Austin, *Sense and Sensibilia*, pp. 15–16.

21 'I say not that there are no other accidents in bodies than colours, odours, and the like: for I have already taught that there are simpler and more primitive affections of matter, from which these secondary qualities, if I may so call them, do depend; and that the operations of bodies upon one another spring from the same.' Robert Boyle, 'The Origin of Forms and Qualities according to the Corpuscular Philosophy' in M.A. Stewart (ed.), *Selected Philosophical Papers of Robert Boyle* (Indianapolis: Hackett Publishing, 1991), p. 32. On the relation between Locke and Boyle see Peter Alexander, *Ideas, Qualities and Corpuscles: Locke and Boyle on the External World* (Cambridge: Cambridge University Press, 1985), *passim*.

22 Galileo Galilei, *The Assayer*, 311.

23 'Take a grain of Wheat, divide it into two parts, each part has still *Solidity, Extension, Figure, and Mobility*; divide it again and it retains still the same qualities; and so divide it on, til the parts become insensible, they must retain still each of them all those qualities . . . These I call *original* or *primary Qualities* of Body, which I think we may observe to produce simple *Ideas in us*' (E II.8.9). For an excellent discussion see Edwin McCann, 'Lockean Mechanism' in Vere Chappel (ed.), *Locke* (Oxford: Oxford University Press, 1998), pp. 242–60.

24 Cottingham et al. (eds), *The Philosophical Writings of Descartes*, v. II, pp. 20–2 (*AT* VII: 30–3).

25 Berkeley's arguments against Locke (and Malebranche) rarely if ever distinguish between 'qualities' and 'ideas of qualities'. The loose identification sometimes unfairly undermines an argument or a position that is far more coherent when this distinction is observed. The identification also has an implicit problem that the Lockean distinction does not. If qualities are ideas, what are they ideas of, and what are ideas if they are not ideas of something?

26 'Elucidation Six' in Malebranche, *Search after Truth*, pp. 569–70.

27 Descartes gives a very famous mechanist account of the bodily mechanism involved in the perception of heat in his early 'Treatise on Man,' in Cottingham et al. (eds), *The Philosophical Writings of Descartes*, v. I: 102 (AT XI 144).

28 This is a debate that is still very much alive among philosophers. Pain has its own sensory system, its own neural pathways, etc. This seems to imply that it has its own distinctive contents or quale. Yet philosophers have argued quite convincingly that 'painfulness is not a quale' and rather many sorts of processes at different levels are involved in experiencing pain. See Austen Clark, 'Painfulness is not a Quale' in Murat Aydede (ed.), *Pain: New Essays on its Nature and the Methodology of its Study* (Cambridge, MA: MIT Press, 2005), pp. 177–97.

29 I am only going to discuss whether Berkeley got Locke right on abstraction in passing. The general consensus is that his reading was uncharitable, but also that Locke made an uncharitable reading easy with his discussion of the abstract, general idea of a triangle in *Essay* IV. See Mackie, *Problems from Locke* (Oxford: Oxford University Press, 1976), pp. 118–21. I do wish at the outset though to distinguish between on the one hand what Mackie refers to as 'selective attention' (i.e., attending to one or another particular features of an idea in the same way one can attend to one or another particular feature of a painting), and on the other hand having an idea just of a particular quality. Berkeley will argue that although we can do the former, we can't do the latter. He seems to have taken over the 'selective attention' model from Locke himself, even though he thought that he had himself discovered selective attention as an explanation of general ideas and Locke viewed abstract ideas exclusively in terms of the latter (see Winkler, *Berkeley: An Interpretation*, 42–3).

30 'Berkeley does not believe that all words signify ideas. And his opposition to the belief runs so deep that even the words that *do* signify ideas are not connected to things in the way that the Lockean picture indicates.' Kenneth Winkler, *Berkeley: An Interpretation* (Oxford: Oxford University Press, 1989), p. 20.

31 E.J. Craig distinguished between three senses of abstract ideas: 1. 'The single property view' or an abstract idea of one quality only; 2. 'The common property view' or an 'abstract idea compounded of ideas which are instantiated by every instance of the concept in question'; and 3. 'the full representation view' where 'the abstract idea contains, it seems, ideas of all the properties of all the instances of the general term in question' (Craig, 'Berkeley's on Attack on Abstract Ideas', *The Philosophical Review* 77:4 (Oct., 1968), pp. 425–29). This is a distinction among ways in which an abstract idea might function. Pappas develops a distinction between four senses of abstract ideas. Type I abstract ideas (which correspond to Craig's first category) are ideas 'of single sensible qualities, rather than of combinations of qualities' (Pappas, *Berkeley's Thought*, 41); Type II abstract ideas (which correspond to Craig's second category) are 'general ideas' of sensible quality categories as opposed to ideas of single sensible qualities (ibid, 42); Type III ideas are

like Type II but 'ideas of bodies rather than of qualities,' (ibid, 43); and Type IV ideas are ideas of the most general types of metaphysical predicates, existence and the like (ibid, 44). Pappas is arranging the ideas in a hierarchy of generality. For my purposes I'm primarily interested in the distinction between Type I and the rest, which I will soon discuss.

32 Warnock, *Berkeley*, p. 100.

33 Many of Berkeley's contemporaries thought that there was no problem in abstracting something in the mind which could not be distinguished in reality. See Winkler, *Berkeley: An Interpretation*, p. 37.

34 To see this move from 'ideas as building blocks' and natural signification to the analogy of 'ideas as words' and arbitrary signification, imagine again that we acquire an idea of 'non-blue stripe'. Does the fact that we can separate the words into 'non', 'blue stripe', 'stri', 'b', 'l', mean that we have correspondent ideas of each? And that each of the ideas has an object? Clearly not.

35 Mackie, *Problems in Locke*, p. 115.

36 A Platonist might argue that precisely what makes a universal idea a universal in part is that it can exist independent of any of its particular instantiations by the imagination: so 'the Good' subsists whether or anyone engages in good actions, and so forth. And furthermore, what makes the ideas particular is the imagination, of which the abstractive process purifies the idea of particular features. But of course Locke held no such view (a view which is fraught with its own problems), and Berkeley's arguments are specifically against Locke.

37 cf. Bolton. Pappas tries to show that Berkeley has different arguments against what Pappas calls Type I abstract ideas (which rest on the fact that we cannot separate the contents of the ideas and are thus impossible to acquire) and the other types of abstract ideas (which do not rest on separability but are impossible as such). On his account, Winkler, Bolton and others tend to view all abstract ideas as impossible in the same sense, and consequently do not differentiate between Berkeley's different arguments. Pappas' objection becomes less of a problem if you view Type I ideas as the first step in acquiring the other types of abstract ideas. Then Berkeley is just arguing against the impossibility of abstract ideas in two directions: they are impossible to acquire, and even if they could be acquired they are impossible as such. See the intricate discussion in Pappas, *Berkeley's Thought*, Ch. 3. See also Walter Ott, 'The Cartesian Context of Berkeley's Attack on Abstracticism', Pacific Philosophical Quarterly 85(4) 2004: 107–424.

38 Winkler, *Berkeley: An Interpretation*, p. 44.

39 Ibid., ch. 1.

40 See Donald Baxter, 'Abstraction, Inseparability, Identity', *Philosophy and Phenomenological Research* 57:2 (June 1997), 307–30.

41 'Locke's great oversight seems to be that he did not Begin wth his Third Book at least that he had not some thought of it at first. Certainly the 2 1st books don't agree wt he says in ye 3d' (*PC* 717).

42 Berkeley connects these issues in his final work *Siris* (*S* 316).

43 As with many of Berkeley's criticisms of Locke's doctrine of abstraction, this also is not really fair as a criticism of Locke's theory of language. See 'Of Particles' E III.7.

44 See the brief but excellent discussion in Howard Robinson (ed. and intro.), *George Berkeley: Principles of Knowledge and Three Dialogues* (Oxford: Oxford University Press, 1996), pp. xviii–xxi.

45 He alludes to Malebranche's discussion of pricking one's finger at *D* II: 179: 'I feel pain, for example, when a thorn pricks my finger; but the hole it makes is not the pain. The hole is in the finger – if it is clearly conceived – and the pain is in the soul, for the soul senses it keenly and is disagreeably modified by it.' Malebranche, *The Search after Truth*, I.10, p. 49.

46 The argument is derived from the 'fourth mode' of Sextus Empiricus: 'the same water that seems hot to a person when poured on inflamed parts seems cold to us.' Sextus Empiricus, *Outlines*, I.xiv.

47 It is also problematic for other reasons. Austin presented a powerful objection (related to the discussion of mediate perception we have considered previously) through the classic example of the stick in the glass of water which appears to be bent. The argument presumes that there is one thing that is always straight but which we perceive as bent. But 'exactly what in this case is supposed to be delusive? What is wrong, what is even faintly surprising, in the idea of a stick being straight but looking bent sometimes? Does anyone suppose that if something is straight, then it jolly well has to look straight at all times and in all circumstances?' Austin, *Sense and Sensibilia*, p. 29.

48 Philonous correctly notes that this is a bad inference: 'And granting that we never hear a Sound but when some Motion is produced in the Air, yet I do not see how you can infer from thence, that the Sound itself is in the Air.'

49 'External light is nothing but a thin fluid substance, whose minute particles being agitated with a brisk motion, and in various manners reflected from the different surfaces of outward objects to the eyes, communicate different motions to the optic nerves; which being propagated to the brain, cause therein various impressions: and these are attended with the sensations of red, blue, yellow, etc.' (*D* II: 186). Locke did not think that light could be definitively shown to be a corpuscle, but he thought any other explanation seemed to fail (*E* IV.2.11). Berkeley also paraphrases Locke's discussion of the ways in which our experiences of colour qualities change as light conditions change at *Essay* II.8.19–21.

50 'I know not how men, who have the same idea under different names, or different ideas under the same name, can in that case talk with one another; any more than a man who, not being blind or deaf, has distinct ideas of the colour of scarlet and the sound of a trumpet, could discourse concerning scarlet colour with the blind man I mentioned in another place, who fancied that the idea of scarlet was like the sound of a trumpet' (*E* II.4.5). Still, since Locke held that we can have ideas of multiple senses, he was committed to resemblances of some sort between the senses. Berkeley attempted to exploit this tension against

Locke in the discussion of Molyneux's problem in the *New Theory of Vision*. But all that is needed for this argument is the difference between hearing and the two senses of sight and touch.

51 The stronger version of the argument is stated clearly in the *Principles*: 'But, say you, though the ideas themselves do not exist without the mind, yet there may be things like them, whereof they are copies or resemblances, which things exist without the mind in an unthinking substance. I answer, an idea can be like nothing but an idea; a colour or figure can be like nothing but another colour or figure. If we look but never so little into our thoughts, we shall find it impossible for us to conceive a likeness except only between our ideas. Again, I ask whether those supposed originals or external things, of which our ideas are the pictures or representations, be themselves perceivable or no? If they are, then they are ideas and we have gained our point; but if you say they are not, I appeal to any one whether it be sense to assert a colour is like something which is invisible; hard or soft, like something which is intangible; and so of the rest' (P 8).

52 P.F. Strawson, 'Causation in Perception' in Strawson, *Freedom and Resentment and Other Essays* (London: Methuen, 1974), p. 79.

53 Gareth Evans, 'Things without Minds' in A. Phillips (ed.), *The Collected Papers of Gareth Evans* (Oxford: Oxford University Press, 1985).

54 Berkeley is very loose here with 'corporeal substance' and 'visible object', as well as with different senses of perception. And why couldn't the corporeal substance be mediately signified by the colours we perceive as on or making up the object?

55 cf. Descartes' invocation of this causal axiom in the proof for God in *Meditations* III.

56 'There is a singer everyone has heard//Loud, a mid-summer and a mid-wood bird// Who makes the solid tree trunks sound again.//He says that leaves are old and that for flowers// Mid-summer is to spring as one to ten.//He says the early petal-fall is past,// When pear and cherry bloom went down in showers// On sunny days a moment overcast;// And comes that other fall we name the fall.//He says the highway dust is over all.//The bird would cease and be as other birds//But that he knows in singing not to sing.//The question that he frames in all but words//Is what to make of a diminished thing.' Robert Frost, 'The Oven Bird'. On the philosophical issue see Margaret Wilson, 'Berkeley on the Mind-Dependence of Colours', *Pacific Philosophical Quarterly* 68 (1987), pp. 249–64.

57 See Margaret Atherton, 'How Berkeley Can Maintain That Snow is White', *Philosophy and Phenomenological Research* 67:1 (July 2003), 101–13.

58 Sellars intended the example as a criticism of sense datum theories. See Wilfred Sellars, 'Empiricism and the Philosopy of Mind,' §14 in Wilfred Sellars, *Science, Perception and Reality* (London: Routledge & Kegan Paul, 1963). See also www.ditext.com/sellars/epm.

59 This strange turn of phrase points to the issue diagnosed previously by Austin. If we are experiencing perceptual variation in what since can we also be perceiving a stable percept?

60 Berkeley appears to be making a sly reference to a passage in the *Essay* where Locke remarks: 'The simple modes of Number are of all other the most distinct . . . the Idea of Two as distinct, from the Idea of Three, as the Magnitude of the whole Earth, is from that of a Mite' (*E* II.16.3).

61 Acceptance or rejection of the thesis that animals were unthinking machines was one of the major dividing lines between some Cartesians (Descartes, Malebranche) and many British philosophers (Hobbes, Boyle, Locke). It does not provide for a good test for whether a philosopher was a 'Continental rationalist' or a 'British empiricist', since both Spinoza and Leibniz held that animals were capable of rudimentary thought.

62 See Nancy Cartwright, *How the Laws of Physics Lie* (Oxford: Oxford University Press, 1983); Ian Hacking, *Representing and Intervening: Introductory Topics in the Philosophy of Science* (Cambridge: Cambridge University Press, 1983).

63 Benoît Mandelbrot, 'How Long Is the Coast of Britain? Statistical Self–Similarity and Fractional Dimension,' *Science* 156 (1967), pp. 636–8. The paper can be downloaded at www.math.yale.edu/mandelbrot/webbooks/wb_top.

64 See, for example Spinoza's thought experiment combining both mite and microscopy: 'the worm in the blood' in Edwin Curley (ed. and trans.), *A Spinoza Reader: The Ethics and Other Works* (Princeton, NJ: Princeton University Press, 1994). On the theme in general see Catherine Wilson, *The Invisible World: Early Modern Philosophy and the Invention of the Microscope* (Princeton, NJ: Princeton University Press, 1995). Fontenelle's *Conversations* belong to this genre as well, imagining what life might be like on other planets, spurred by the invention of the telescope. On Berkeley in particular see Geneviève Brykman, 'Microscopes and Philosophical Method in Berkeley' in Turbayne (ed.), *Berkeley: Critical and Interpretive Essays*, pp. 69–82; Margaret Wilson, 'Berkeley on the Mind-dependence of Colours'; Bruce Silver, 'The conflicting Microscopic worlds of Berkeley's *Three Dialogues,*' *Journal of the History of Ideas* 37 (1976), 343–9; Robert W. Faaborg, 'Berkeley and the Argument from Microscopes', *Pacific Philosophical Quarterly* 80 (1999) 301–23. I will return to the question of microscopes in the discussion of the 'Third Dialogue'.

65 In the *Novum Organum* and a host of other works, Bacon (1561–1626) outlined a vast research programme for the natural and human sciences. He was the main ideologist of early modern scientific culture and influenced most of the major early modern natural philosophers, either directly (Hobbes was his secretary) or indirectly.

66 'And it will be an unpardonable, as well as Childish Peevishness, if we undervalue the Advantages of our Knowledge, and neglect to improve it to the ends for which it was given us, because there are some Things that are set out of the reach of it . . . [if we] intemperately require Demonstration, and demand certainty, where Probabilty only is to be had, and which is sufficient to govern all our Concernments . . . we

shall do much – what as wisely as he, who would not use his Legs, but sit still and perish, because he had no Wings to fly' (E I.1.5).

67 Isaac Newton, *Philosophia Naturalis Principia Mathematica* (1676), 'Scholium to the Definitions'. Berkeley paraphrases this passage in *P* 111.

68 M. Hughes, 'Newton, Hermes, and Berkeley', *British Journal of the Philosophy of Science* 43 (1992), 1–19.

69 G.J. Whitrow claimed that Berkeley had an essential insight in *De Motu* (*DM* 59), which responded to a problem in defining absolute space (that it still seemed to depend on one body as a fixed reference point), and anticipated Ernst Mach (and by extension Einstein). The insight was that 'no *one* star should be regarded as more favoured than any other and hence that reference should be made to the framework of *all.*' G.J. Whitrow, 'Berkeley's Philosophy of Motion', *The British Journal for the Philosophy of Science*, 4:13 (May 1953), p. 43.

70 The term 'substance' is old as philosophy, going back to the Greek term *ousia*, which was derived from the Greek verb for being, and which meant inheritance as well as substance. Substance is the central concept in Aristotle's metaphysics, and Aristotle interpreters struggle over the same questions that Locke interpreters do in making sense of the concept. Is substance identified with universals? With natural kind terms? With individuals? With an underlying subject of predication? For Aristotle substance is connected with, and perhaps identified with, formal and final cause, which makes substances connected to teleology in a way that would be at odds with the new science and the Royal Society. Berkeley did not reject teleology.

71 Jonathan Bennett has strongly rejected this identification, claiming that it arises from Berkeley's confusion between Locke's theory of substance and the so-called 'veil of perception' doctrine (that ideas are a veil or intermediary between our minds and a reality we never directly perceive). For example, G.J. Warnock sees the veil of perception issue, or 'duplication of the world', as at the heart of Berkeley's rejection of Lockean material substance (Warnock, *Berkeley*, p. 101). According to Bennett the distinction must be maintained, since 'The former tries to say what concepts we use when we say *Something is F*, while the latter has to do with the difference between *I see a tree* and *It is as though I were seeing a tree.*' Jonathan Bennett, *Locke, Berkeley, Hume: Central Themes* (Oxford: Clarendon Press, 1971), p. 70. Bennett points out, though, that Berkeley does not reject substance as such, only material substance, because he uses substance when analyzing spiritual substances (ibid., pp. 86–7).

72 See *Principles* §§ 1, 2, 17, and 49 for further discussion. See also Phillip D. Cummins, 'Berkeley on minds and agency' in Winkler, *Cambridge Companion to Berkeley*, pp. 209–19.

73 See D.M. Armstrong, *Berkeley's Theory of Vision: A Critical Examination of Bishop Berkeley's Essay towards a New Theory of Vision* (Melbourne: Melbourne University Press, 1960); Margaret Atherton,

Berkeley's Revolution in Vision (Ithaca: Cornell University Press, 1990), and 'Berkeley's Theory of Vision and its Reception' in Winkler (ed.), *The Cambridge Companion to Berkeley*, pp. 94–124.

74 The term was coined by Andre Gallois in his insightful paper 'Berkeley's Master Argument', *Philosophical Review* 83:1 (1974), pp. 55–69.

75 Thanks to Corliss Swain for explaining this passage to me.

76 George Pitcher, *Berkeley* (London: Routledge & Kegan Paul, 1977), p. 159.

77 Thanks to Walter Hopp for this objection.

78 For an extensive discussion of these methodological issues see Aaron Garrett, *Meaning in Spinoza's Method* (Cambridge: Cambridge University Press, 2003).

79 'Second Objections and Replies.'

80 Hume would soon provide the most famous account of this in *A Treatise* I. IV.7, when after being caught in sceptical reflections he returned to common life: 'I dine, I play a game of backgammon, I converse, and am merry with my friends; and when after three or four hours' amusement, I wou'd return to these speculations, they appear so cold, and strain'd, and ridiculous, that I cannot find it in my heart to enter them any farther.'

81 Hume – who as I have been stressing throughout was deeply influenced by Berkeley while taking Berkeley's arguments in directions which would have scandalized him even more than Hobbes and Spinoza did – recognized that there is an important ambiguity in how we use the word 'nature' (T 3.1.2). Sometimes we use it in opposition to miraculous ('Cloning isn't a miracle, if you understand how it works it's perfectly natural'); sometimes in opposition to rare ('That's the natural response to someone cursing at you, but Gandhi had wisdom far beyond what was natural'); and sometimes in opposition to artificial ('Cloning is an artificial procedure wholly at odds with natural childbirth').

82 cf. Spinoza, *Ethics*, V 'Introduction'.

83 This criticism is a very brisk presentation of eliminativism built on the 'theory-ladeness' of observation. See Daniel Dennett, 'Why You Can't Make a Computer that Feels Pain' in *Brainstorms* (Cambridge, MA: MIT Press, 1978), Ch. 11.

84 For Epicureans, ideas of sense were *literally* thin: thin films or *simulacra*, which rapidly peeled and then floated off the object into our sense organs.

85 'Inquiry Concerning Virtue' II.1 in Shaftesbury, *Characteristics*.

86 See Margaret Atherton, 'Berkeley's Theory of Vision and its Reception' in Winkler (ed.), *The Cambridge Companion to Berkeley*, Ch. 4.

87 There are problems with the analogy as well, beginning with the fact that it is a language that is spoken to us and that we do not speak. For a detailed discussion see David Berman, *George Berkeley: Idealist and the Man* (Oxford: Clarendon Press, 1994), Ch. 6.

88 Spinoza, *Ethics*, I.12.

89 Section VI in Samuel Clarke, *A Demonstration of the Being and Attributes of God and Other Writings*, Ezio Vailati (ed.) (Cambridge: Cambridge University Press, 1998), 33.

90 Clarke, *A Demonstration*, 96.

91 A few pages later he offers another, similar argument: 'It is evident that the Things I perceive are my own ideas, and that no idea can exist unless it be in a mind. Nor is it less plain that these ideas or things by me perceived, either themselves or their archetypes, exist independently of my mind, since I know myself not to be their author, it being out of my power to determine at pleasure, what particular ideas I shall be affected with upon opening my eyes or ears. They must therefore exist in some other mind, whose will it is they should be exhibited to me. The things, I say, immediately perceived, are ideas or sensations, call them which you will. But how can any idea or sensation exist in, or be produced by, any thing but a mind or spirit?'

92 See particularly his *Treatise on Nature and Grace* (1680).

93 This was the position of Berkeley's admirer and critic Thomas Reid.

94 For a sophisticated account of Berkeley on relative notions in particular and notions in general, see Daniel Flage, *Berkeley's Doctrine of Notions: A Reconstruction Based on His Theory of Meaning* (London: Croom Helm, 1987).

95 Atherton, 'How Berkeley can maintain that snow is white,' p. 111.

96 Or is this red and tasty?' 'I see this cherry. I feel it, I taste it: and I am sure nothing cannot be seen, or felt, or tasted: It is therefore real. Take away the sensations of softness, moisture, redness, tartness, and you take away the cherry. Since it is not a being distinct from sensations; a cherry, I say, is nothing but a congeries of sensible impressions, or ideas perceived by various senses: Which ideas are united into one thing (or have one name given them) by the mind; because they are observed to attend each other.' (*D* II: 249).

97 See Cicero, *On Academic Scepticism*, Charles Brittan (trans. and ed.), (Indianapolis: Hackett Publishing, 2006), p. 46.

98 See Phillip Cummins, 'Hylas' Parity Argument' in Turbayne (ed.), *Berkeley: Critical and Interpretive Essays*, pp. 283–95.

99 See Pitcher, *Berkeley*, Ch. 10 for a fine-toothed discussion of the problems involved.

100 See Winkler, Berkeley: *An Interpretation*, Ch. 9.

101 Malebranche, *Search For Truth*, III.1.1

102 See C.C.W. Taylor, 'Action and Inaction in Berkeley' in Howard Robinson and John Foster (eds.), *Essays on Berkeley: A Terecentennial Celebration* (Oxford: Clarendon Press, 1985), pp. 211–25.

103 See, particularly, Robert Imlay, 'Berkeley on Action' in Robert G. Muehlmann, (ed.), *Berkeley's Metaphysics: Structural Interpretive and Critical Essays* (State College, PA: Penn State Press, 1995), pp. 171–82; Catherine Wilson, 'On Imlay's 'Berkeley and Action', pp. 183–96.

104 See Patrick Fleming, 'Berkeley's Immaterialist Account of Action', *Journal of the History of Philosophy* 44: 3 (2006), pp. 415–29.

105 Hughes, 'Newton, Hermes, Berkeley'.

INDEX

CPSIA information can be obtained at www.ICGtesting.com
Printed in the USA
LVOW07s2307090116

469918LV00014B/358/P